Taste of Home's
Budget Suppers

PICTURED ABOVE AND ON COVER. Cheddar Corn Bread, Skillet Chicken Supper and Chocolate Potato Cake (recipes on pages 42-43).

PICTURED ON BACK COVER. Grilled Meat Loaf, Beans with Parsley Sauce and Peanut Butter Pudding Pie (recipes on pages 10-11).

Dish Out Down-Home Meals... Not a Lot of Money!

With today's high prices, going out to sit-down restaurants, picking up fast food at the drive-thru and buying prepared dinners in the frozen food section of the grocery store aren't the most economical ways to feed your family supper...nor are they the most satisfying.

Taste of Home's Budget Suppers contains 52 family-pleasing menus you can prepare right in your own kitchen. Each complete meal calls for basic ingredients you most likely have on hand in the pantry, refrigerator or freezer, so they're easy on the pocketbook, especially compared to those more costly dinner solutions!

Cost-conscious cooks from across the country shared these frugal yet flavorful family recipes. Our home economists taste-tested each dish as well, then figured the cost per serving, which is included with each down-home supper.

Grilled Meat Loaf, Beans with Parsley Sauce and Peanut Butter Pudding Pie (pages 10-11) make a great-tasting meal perfect for the warm spring and summer months that won't burn a hole in your wallet...in fact, it costs just 99¢ a plate!

Come crisp autumn days, you'll warm the kitchen as well as your family's hearts with homey Pineapple Ham Loaf, Broccoli Cream Soup and Buttermilk Rolls (pages 28-29) for just $1.51 per serving.

Holiday shopping might put a strain on your budget, but serving your family Cranberry Turkey Loaf, Glazed Sprouts and Carrots and Mock Apple Pie (pages 60-61) won't...it's just 95¢ a person.

That's just a small sample of the 52 complete meals—156 recipes in all—compiled on the following pages. You can also mix and match the recipes to come up with countless money-saving menus—enough for every day of the year and then some.

So pass by the drive-thru and grocery store, and forget making dinner reservations...with *Taste of Home's Budget Suppers*, you can serve your family penny-pinching meals without scrimping on flavor!

Editor: Jean Steiner
Art Directors: Catherine Fletcher, Kathy Crawford
Associate Editors: Beth Wittlinger, Heidi Reuter Lloyd
Food Editor: Janaan Cunningham
Associate Food Editors: Coleen Martin, Diane Werner
Senior Recipe Editor: Sue A. Jurack
Recipe Editor: Janet Briggs
Food Photography: Rob Hagen, Dan Roberts
Food Photography Artists: Julie Ferron, Sue Myers
Photo Studio Manager: Anne Schimmel
Senior Vice President, Editor in Chief: Catherine Cassidy
President: Barbara Newton
Chairman and Founder: Roy Reiman

A Taste of What's Inside!

Pages 12-13

Pages 52-53

Pages 78-79

Pages 64-65

Even if the holidays squeeze your household budget, you can still leave the table satisfied.

Three frugal cooks prove it with this delicious dinner. Our Test Kitchen home economists estimate the total cost at just $1.61 per serving.

Hash Brown Pork Bake is a comforting family-style casserole Darlis Wilfer of Phelps, Wisconsin makes with convenient frozen hash browns.

Caraway, onion, bacon and chicken broth dress up Braised Brussels Sprouts, shared by Yvonne Anderson of New Philadelphia, Ohio.

With its luscious chocolate icing and minty whipped cream filling, Chocolate Mint Layer Cake from Jean Portwine of Recluse, Wyoming makes a fitting finale to a special meal.

$1.61 Per Serving

Hash Brown Pork Bake

    2 cups (16 ounces) sour cream
    1 can (10-3/4 ounces) condensed cream
        of chicken soup, undiluted
    1 package (32 ounces) frozen cubed hash
        brown potatoes, thawed
    2 cups cubed cooked pork
    1 pound process cheese (Velveeta),
        cubed
    1/4 cup chopped onion
    2 cups crushed cornflakes
    1/2 cup stick margarine, melted
    1 cup (4 ounces) shredded mozzarella
        cheese
    3 green pepper rings

In a bowl, combine sour cream and soup. Stir in hash browns, pork, process cheese and onion. Transfer to a greased 3-qt. baking dish. Toss cornflake crumbs and margarine; sprinkle over top.

Bake, uncovered, at 350° for 50 minutes. Sprinkle with mozzarella cheese. Bake 10 minutes longer or until bubbly. Garnish with green pepper. **Yield:** 8 servings.

Braised Brussels Sprouts

    2 pounds fresh brussels sprouts
    2 bacon strips, diced
    1 medium onion, chopped
    1 cup chicken broth
    1 teaspoon caraway seeds
    1/4 teaspoon salt
    1/8 teaspoon pepper

Trim the brussels sprouts and cut an "X" in the core of each. Place in a saucepan and cover with water; bring to a boil. Cook for 8-10 minutes or until crisp-tender. Meanwhile, in a large skillet, cook the bacon until crisp; remove with a slotted spoon to paper towels.

Saute onion in the drippings until tender. Stir in the broth, caraway seeds, salt and pepper. Simmer, uncovered, until liquid has almost evaporated. Drain sprouts. Add sprouts and bacon to onion mixture; toss to combine. **Yield:** 8 servings.

Chocolate Mint Layer Cake

    1/2 cup butter, softened
    1-3/4 cups sugar
        3 eggs
        4 squares (1 ounce *each*) unsweetened
            chocolate, melted and cooled
        1 teaspoon vanilla extract
    3/4 cup milk
    1/2 cup water
    1-3/4 cups all-purpose flour
    3/4 teaspoon baking soda

1/2 teaspoon salt
FILLING:
  1 cup heavy whipping cream
  3 tablespoons confectioners' sugar
  1/8 teaspoon peppermint extract
  3 to 4 drops green food coloring, optional
ICING:
  1 cup (6 ounces) semisweet chocolate
    chips
  1/4 cup butter
  1/3 cup evaporated milk
  1 teaspoon vanilla extract
1-1/2 cups confectioners' sugar

Line two greased 9-in. round baking pans with waxed paper. Grease and flour paper; set aside. In a mixing bowl, cream butter and sugar. Beat in eggs one at a time, beating well after each addition.

Beat in chocolate and vanilla.

Combine milk and water. Combine the flour, baking soda and salt; add to creamed mixture alternately with milk mixture. Pour into prepared pans. Bake at 350° for 24-28 minutes or until a toothpick comes out clean. Cool for 10 minutes before removing from pans to wire racks.

For filling, in a mixing bowl, beat the cream until it begins to thicken. Add confectioners' sugar and extract; beat until stiff peaks form. Beat in food coloring if desired. Place one cake layer on a serving plate; spread with filling. Top with second cake.

For icing, in a microwave-safe mixing bowl, melt chips and butter; cool slightly. Beat in evaporated milk and vanilla. Gradually beat in confectioners' sugar. Frost and decorate cake. Chill 2 hours before slicing. **Yield:** 12 servings.

Dishing out hearty helpings of down-home foods doesn't mean you also have to dish out hoards of money.

Our Test Kitchen home economists have combined the recipes here from three budget-minded cooks into a delicious and satisfying meal you can put on the table for just $1.50 per person.

Hay and Straw is not only quick and easy to prepare, it's pretty, too. This colorful pasta dish combines julienned ham, Parmesan cheese, peas and linguine.

"The trick is to have all the ingredients ready at the same time, so you can toss it all together without having to reheat," says Priscilla Weaver of Hagerstown, Maryland.

Bits of crumbled bacon add texture to Creamy Bacon Salad Dressing from DeEtta Rasmussen of Fort Madison, Iowa. With a mayonnaise and vinegar base, this thick, slightly tangy blend coats tossed greens or spinach nicely.

"Chocolate Cream Dessert makes a cool and delicious treat on a warm summer day or any time of year," says Pam Reddell of Linden, Wisconsin. "I bake a tender crust from a cake mix, then layer it with a cream cheese blend, chocolate pudding and whipped topping."

$1.50 Per Person

Hay and Straw

  1 **package (16 ounces) linguine**
  2 **cups julienned fully cooked ham**
  1 **tablespoon butter**
  3 **cups frozen peas**
1-1/2 **cups shredded Parmesan cheese**
  1/3 **cup heavy whipping cream**

Cook linguine according to package directions. Meanwhile, in a large skillet, saute ham in butter for 3 minutes. Add peas; heat through.

Drain linguine; toss with ham mixture, Parmesan cheese and cream. Serve immediately. **Yield:** 8 servings.

Creamy Bacon Salad Dressing

1/2 **cup mayonnaise**
  2 **tablespoons cider vinegar**
  2 **tablespoons light corn syrup**
1/8 **teaspoon salt**
  4 **bacon slices, cooked and crumbled**
  2 **tablespoons finely chopped onion**
  6 **cups torn mixed salad greens**

In a small bowl, whisk the mayonnaise, vinegar, corn syrup and salt until smooth. Stir in the bacon and onion. Cover and refrigerate for at least 2 hours. Serve dressing over salad greens. **Yield:** 8 servings (3/4 cup dressing).

Chocolate Cream Dessert

3/4 **cup cold butter**
  1 **package (18-1/4 ounces) chocolate cake mix**
  1 **egg, lightly beaten**
  1 **package (8 ounces) cream cheese, softened**
  1 **cup confectioners' sugar**
  4 **cups whipped topping,** *divided*
  3 **cups cold milk**
  2 **packages (3.9 ounces** *each***) instant chocolate pudding mix**
  2 **tablespoons chocolate curls**

In a large bowl, cut the butter into the cake mix until the mixture resembles coarse crumbs. Add the

egg and mix well. Press into a greased 13-in. x 9-in. x 2-in. baking dish. Bake at 350° for 15-18 minutes or until set. Cool completely in dish on a wire rack.

In a small mixing bowl, beat cream cheese on medium speed until fluffy. Add confectioners' sugar and beat until smooth. Fold in 1 cup of the whipped topping. Carefully spread over the crust; cover and refrigerate until set.

In a large bowl, combine the milk and pudding mix by whisking with a wire whisk for 2 minutes; let stand for 5 minutes or until slightly thickened. Spread over the cream cheese layer. Top with the remaining whipped topping.

Refrigerate for at least 2 hours before cutting. Garnish with chocolate curls. Store leftovers in the refrigerator. **Yield:** 12 servings.

Chocolate Curls

Try a sweet twist—garnish your dessert with chocolate curls!

If you have a solid block of chocolate, simply use a vegetable peeler to peel off curls, allowing them to fall gently onto a plate or piece of waxed paper in a single layer. If you get only shavings, try warming the chocolate just slightly.

Gently slide a toothpick or a wooden skewer through the center of each chocolate curl to carefully lift it onto the dessert and arrange the curls as desired.

You don't have to "shell out" a lot of money on grocery bills when feeding your family.

The recipes here are suggested by three budget-minded cooks and combined by our Test Kitchen staff into a delicious meal you can serve for just $1.56 per person.

Three-Cheese Shells make a hearty meatless entree. "It's easy to prepare ahead, then bake just in time for dinner," says June Barrus of Springville, Utah.

Bacon, brown sugar and cider vinegar season Beans 'n' Caramelized Onions. "I often serve this dish to guests, and it never fails to please," shares Jill Heatwole from Pittsville, Maryland.

With a tangy filling and a nutmeg-flavored crust, Lemon Cheese Squares hit the spot after a meal or as a snack. "My grandmother made these bars for me when I was growing up, and they were my favorite," recalls Emily Weedman of Milwaukie, Oregon.

Three-Cheese Shells

   1 package (12 ounces) jumbo pasta shells
   3 cups (24 ounces) ricotta cheese
   3 cups (12 ounces) shredded mozzarella
      cheese
1/2 cup grated Parmesan cheese
1/2 cup chopped green pepper
1/2 cup chopped fresh mushrooms
   2 tablespoons dried basil
   2 eggs, lightly beaten
   2 garlic cloves, minced
1/2 teaspoon seasoned salt
1/4 teaspoon pepper
   2 jars (one 28 ounces, one 14 ounces)
      spaghetti sauce, *divided*

Cook pasta shells according to package directions. Drain and rinse in cold water. In a bowl, combine the next 10 ingredients. Divide the small jar of spaghetti sauce between two ungreased 13-in. x 9-in. x 2-in. baking dishes.

Fill pasta shells with the cheese mixture and place in a single layer over sauce. Pour the remaining spaghetti sauce over the shells. Cover and bake at 350° for 20 minutes. Uncover and bake 10 minutes longer or until heated through. **Yield:** 9 servings.

Beans 'n' Caramelized Onions

   4 bacon strips
   2 large onions, cut lengthwise
      into 1/2-inch-thick wedges
   2 pounds fresh green beans, trimmed
   3 tablespoons cider vinegar
4-1/2 teaspoons brown sugar

$1.56 Per Serving

1/4 teaspoon salt
1/4 teaspoon pepper

In a skillet, cook bacon over medium heat until crisp. Remove to paper towels. Drain, reserving 2 tablespoons drippings. Crumble bacon and set aside. In drippings, cook onions over medium-low heat until tender and golden brown, about 50 minutes.

Meanwhile, place the beans in a large saucepan and cover with water; bring to a boil. Cook, uncovered, for 8-10 minutes or until crisp-tender. Drain. Stir the vinegar and brown sugar into onions; add beans. Cook, uncovered, over medium heat for 1 minute. Add bacon; toss gently. Season with salt and pepper. **Yield:** 9 servings.

Lemon Cheese Squares

1/3 cup stick margarine, softened
1/4 cup packed brown sugar
  1 cup all-purpose flour
1/4 teaspoon salt
1/4 teaspoon ground nutmeg
FILLING:
  1 cup (8 ounces) small-curd cottage
    cheese
  1 egg
  1 egg white
  3 tablespoons lemon juice
  1 cup sugar
  2 tablespoons all-purpose flour

1 tablespoon grated lemon peel
1/4 teaspoon baking powder

In a mixing bowl, cream margarine and brown sugar. Combine flour, salt and nutmeg; add to creamed mixture. Press into a greased 8-in. square baking dish. Bake at 350° for 18-20 minutes until golden brown.

For filling, place cottage cheese, egg, egg white and lemon juice in a blender or food processor. Cover; process until smooth. Add the sugar, flour, lemon peel and baking powder. Cover; process until blended. Pour over crust. Bake at 350° for 30-34 minutes until edges are lightly browned. Cool on a wire rack 1 hour. Refrigerate until chilled. **Yield:** 9 servings.

Fire up the grill for this great-tasting meal that won't burn a hole in your pocketbook.

It combines three frugal yet flavorful recipes from fellow cost-conscious cooks. Our Test Kitchen staff estimates the total price at just 99¢ per serving!

Grilled Meat Loaf is the perfect summertime twist on a comforting family favorite. Catherine Carpenter of Barnesville, Ohio shapes the meat mixture into loaves and "bakes" them on the grill. Ketchup brushed over the meat lends a little sweetness to each slice.

You'll likely find the main ingredient for Beans with Parsley Sauce right in your garden. For a bit of extra color, try mixing wax beans with green beans. Veronica Teipel of Manchester, Missouri shares the recipe, saying, "The flavor is definitely worth the preparation time."

Peanut Butter Pudding Pie, from Valerie Sisson of Norton, Ohio, is pretty enough to serve company...if your family doesn't get to it first! No one will be able to resist a sweet piece of this creamy chocolate and peanut butter dessert.

99¢ Per Person

Grilled Meat Loaf

1/2 cup ketchup
1/2 cup quick-cooking oats
1/4 cup chopped green pepper
1 egg
1 teaspoon dried parsley flakes
1 teaspoon Worcestershire sauce
1/2 teaspoon garlic powder
1/2 teaspoon dried basil
1/4 teaspoon pepper
2 pounds ground beef
Additional ketchup, optional

In a large bowl, combine the first nine ingredients. Crumble ground beef over mixture and mix well. Shape into two loaves. Place a sheet of heavy-duty foil in center of grill. Place the meat loaves on foil (do not seal foil).

Grill, covered, over indirect medium heat for 50 minutes or until meat is no longer pink and a meat thermometer reads 160°. Brush tops with additional ketchup if desired. Let stand for 10 minutes before slicing. **Yield:** 2 loaves (4 servings each).

Beans with Parsley Sauce

2 pounds fresh green beans, trimmed
2 tablespoons butter
2 tablespoons all-purpose flour
1 teaspoon salt
1/8 teaspoon pepper
1-1/2 cups chicken broth
2 egg yolks

1/2 cup milk
1 cup minced fresh parsley

Place beans in a large saucepan and cover with water; bring to a boil. Cook, uncovered, for 8-10 minutes or until crisp tender. Meanwhile, in a large skillet, melt butter over medium heat. Stir in the flour, salt and pepper until smooth. Gradually whisk in broth. Bring to a boil; cook and stir for 1-2 minutes or until thickened. Remove from the heat.

In a small bowl, combine egg yolks and milk. Stir a small amount of hot broth mixture into egg mixture. Return all to the pan, stirring constantly. Bring to a gentle boil; cook and stir for 2 minutes or until thickened. Stir in parsley. Drain beans; top with sauce. **Yield:** 8 servings.

Peanut Butter Pudding Pie

2 cups milk
1 package (3 ounces) cook-and-serve
vanilla pudding mix
1 cup peanut butter chips
1 graham cracker crust (9 inches)
2-1/2 cups whipped topping
1/3 cup milk chocolate chips
1 teaspoon shortening

In a saucepan, whisk the milk and pudding mix. Cook and stir over medium heat until mixture comes to a boil.

Reduce heat; stir in the peanut butter chips until melted. Pour into the crust. Cover and refrigerate for 3-4 hours or until set.

Spread whipped topping over pie. In a microwave-safe bowl, melt chocolate chips and shortening. Cool for 5 minutes. Drizzle over topping. Refrigerate until serving. **Yield:** 8 servings.

PB Pointer
Did you know that peanut butter was promoted as a health food at the 1904 St. Louis World's Fair? Unopened, it can be stored in a cool, dry place for 1 year; once opened, about 3 months.

You can be frugal and still prepare a satisfying, full-flavored fall dinner for your family. Three budget-conscious cooks prove it with these penny-pinching yet palate-pleasing recipes.

Our Test Kitchen home economists estimate the total cost for this meal is just $1.35 a serving!

When there's a chill in the air, nothing beats Slow Cooker Beef Stew from Earnestine Wilson of Waco, Texas. Seasoned with thyme and ground mustard, the hearty slow-cooked stew is chock-full of tender carrots, potatoes and beef.

Yellow Squash Muffins are so moist and golden, they're sure to become an instant family favorite. The muffins, shared by Doris Heath of Franklin, North Carolina, have a delicate squash flavor.

"I love to bake and experiment with ingredients," says Kathy Roberts of New Hebron, Mississippi. "Sometimes I get lucky and produce something that's new and tasty, like Sweet Potato Custard Pie."

$1.35 Per Serving

Slow Cooker Beef Stew

1-1/2 pounds potatoes, peeled and cubed
6 medium carrots, cut into 1-inch slices
1 medium onion, coarsely chopped
3 celery ribs, coarsely chopped
3 tablespoons all-purpose flour
1-1/2 pounds beef stew meat, cut into 1-inch cubes
3 tablespoons vegetable oil
1 can (14-1/2 ounces) diced tomatoes, undrained
1 cup beef broth
1 teaspoon ground mustard
1/2 teaspoon salt
1/2 teaspoon pepper
1/2 teaspoon dried thyme
1/2 teaspoon browning sauce

Layer the potatoes, carrots, onion and celery in a 5-qt. slow cooker. Place flour in a large resealable plastic bag. Add stew meat; seal and toss to coat evenly. In a large skillet, brown meat in oil in batches. Place over vegetables.

In a large bowl, combine tomatoes, broth, mustard, salt, pepper, thyme and browning sauce. Pour over beef. Cover; cook on high for 1-1/2 hours. Reduce heat to low; cook 7-8 hours longer or until meat and vegetables are tender. **Yield:** 8 servings.

Yellow Squash Muffins

1 pound yellow summer squash, cut into 1-inch slices
1/2 cup butter, melted
1 egg, lightly beaten
1-1/2 cups all-purpose flour
1/2 cup sugar
2-1/2 teaspoons baking powder
1/2 teaspoon salt

Place 1 in. of water in a saucepan; add squash. Bring to a boil. Reduce heat; cover and simmer for 5 minutes or until tender. Drain and mash; stir in the butter and egg. In a bowl, combine the flour, sugar, baking powder and salt. Stir in the squash mixture just until moistened.

Fill greased muffin cups three-fourths full. Bake at 375° for 20-25 minutes or until a toothpick comes out clean. Cool for 5 minutes before removing from pan to a wire rack. **Yield:** 1 dozen.

Sweet Potato Custard Pie

2 small sweet potatoes, peeled and chopped
3/4 cup marshmallow creme
1/2 cup butter, cubed
1 can (5 ounces) evaporated milk
3 eggs
1 teaspoon vanilla extract
1/4 teaspoon almond extract
3/4 cup sugar
1/4 cup packed brown sugar
1 tablespoon all-purpose flour
1/8 teaspoon ground cinnamon
1/8 teaspoon ground nutmeg
1 unbaked pastry shell (9 inches)
1/2 cup whipped topping

Place sweet potatoes in a large saucepan; cover with water. Bring to a boil. Reduce heat; cover and simmer for 10 minutes or until tender. Drain potatoes and place in a large mixing bowl; mash. Add marshmallow creme and butter; beat until smooth. Add milk, eggs and extracts; mix well.

Combine the sugars, flour, cinnamon and nutmeg; gradually beat into potato mixture until well blended. Pour into pastry shell. Bake at 350° for 45-50 minutes or until a knife comes out clean. Cool on a wire rack. Serve with whipped topping. Refrigerate leftovers. **Yield:** 8 servings.

Can you eat well around the holidays without breaking the family grocery budget? You bet.

This down-home dinner is tasty, filling, colorful and economical. The recipes come from three terrific cooks, two who live on opposite coasts and one from just about in the middle.

Our Test Kitchen home economists estimate the cost at just $1.62 per setting, which will come in handy when you're trying to save money to go Christmas shopping. In fact, this menu will be appreciated any time of year—it's that good.

Swiss Pot Roast is suggested by Darlene Markel of Salem, Oregon. "My family loves the taste of this tender roast," says Darlene. "I love the fact that it's so easy to prepare—it even makes its own gravy. The house smells wonderful when this hearty main dish is cooking, so 'How long until dinner?' is apt to be asked."

Cucumbers in Cream is a five-ingredient salad that goes together quick as a wink. The refreshing recipe comes from Dolores Hayes of Fort Plain, New York who notes, "This salad is a great way to use locally produced cream."

And just to show that even a budget-conscious meal can have a festive finale, Katherine Kuhlemeier of Pearl City, Illinois shares her recipe for Homemade Eggnog Pie. "It's rich and scrumptious," she promises.

$1.62 Per Person

Swiss Pot Roast

1 **boneless beef chuck roast (3 pounds)**
1 **tablespoon vegetable oil**
8 **medium potatoes, peeled and quartered**
8 **medium carrots, cut into chunks**
1 **medium onion, sliced**
3 **tablespoons all-purpose flour**
1 **cup water**
1 **can (8 ounces) tomato sauce**
1 **teaspoon beef bouillon granules**
1/2 **teaspoon salt**
1/2 **teaspoon pepper**

In a Dutch oven, brown the roast on all sides in oil; drain. Add the potatoes, carrots and onion. In a bowl, combine the flour, water, tomato sauce, beef bouillon granules, salt and pepper; mix until smooth. Pour over the roast and vegetables.

Cover and bake at 325° for about 2-1/2 to 3 hours or until the meat and vegetables are tender. **Yield:** 8 servings.

Cucumbers in Cream

1/4 **cup white vinegar**
1 **cup heavy whipping cream**
5 **medium cucumbers, sliced**
1/4 **teaspoon salt**
1/8 **teaspoon pepper**

In a large bowl, gradually whisk the vinegar into the cream. Gently stir in the cucumbers, salt and pepper. Serve immediately or refrigerate for a short time. Serve with a slotted spoon. **Yield:** 8 servings.

Homemade Eggnog Pie

1-1/8 **teaspoons unflavored gelatin**
1/4 **cup cold water**
3/4 **cup sugar**
2 **tablespoons cornstarch**
2/3 **cup milk**
3 **egg yolks, lightly beaten**

1 teaspoon vanilla extract
1-1/2 cups heavy whipping cream, whipped
1 pastry shell (9 inches), baked
1/8 teaspoon ground nutmeg

In a small bowl, soften gelatin in cold water; set aside. In a saucepan, combine sugar and cornstarch. Gradually stir in milk until smooth. Bring to a boil; cook and stir for 2 minutes or until thickened. Remove from the heat. Stir a small amount of hot mixture into egg yolks. Return all to the pan; bring to a gentle boil, stirring constantly.

Remove from the heat; stir in gelatin and vanilla. Cool to room temperature, stirring occasionally. Fold in whipped cream. Pour into pie shell. Sprinkle with nutmeg. Refrigerate until set, about 2 hours. **Yield:** 8 servings.

Whipping Cream

The bowl in which you whip cream should be deep enough so the cream can double in volume.

Cream will whip faster if you chill the bowl and beaters in the freezer for 15 minutes. The cream should also be as cold as possible.

Have you ever wondered why whipping cream whips and milk doesn't? The reason is that cream has a higher fat content.

When the cream is whipped, the fat globules cluster together in the bubble walls, forming a network that holds air.

Not only is the comforting meal featured here full of kid-appeal, it's approved by budget-minded cooks, too!

Three such cooks suggested the fun yet frugal recipes. Our Test Kitchen staff then combined them into one family-pleasing meal you can serve for just 99¢ per person!

Slow-Cooked Mac 'n' Cheese is a classic casserole kids of all ages will fall for. "It's a rich and cheesy meatless main dish," notes Bernice Glascoe of Roxboro, North Carolina. "I've never met anyone who didn't ask for second helpings of this cheese-filled dish."

Sunflower Broccoli has great flavor and a nice crunch. The easy recipe is from Jean Artus of Aurora, Colorado. Even kids who don't normally care for broccoli will gobble it up.

Since chocolate and peanut butter are two of her granddaughters' favorite flavors, Elaine Medeiros of Wamego, Kansas frequently fixes Peanut Butter Chocolate Cake as a finale to her meals. "It's both moist and scrumptious," assures Elaine.

99¢ Per Serving

Slow-Cooked Mac 'n' Cheese

1 package (16 ounces) elbow macaroni, uncooked
1/2 cup stick margarine, melted
2 eggs, beaten
1 can (12 ounces) evaporated milk
1 can (10-3/4 ounces) condensed cheddar cheese soup, undiluted
1 cup milk
4 cups (16 ounces) shredded cheddar cheese, *divided*
1/8 teaspoon paprika

Cook the macaroni according to package directions and drain. Place in a 5-qt. slow cooker; add the margarine.

In a bowl, combine the eggs, evaporated milk, soup, milk and 3 cups cheese. Pour over macaroni mixture; stir to combine. Cover and cook on low for 4 hours.

Sprinkle with the remaining cheese. Cook 15 minutes longer or until cheese is melted. Sprinkle with paprika. **Yield:** 10 servings.

Sunflower Broccoli

✓ Uses less fat, sugar or salt. Includes Nutritional Analysis and Diabetic Exchanges.

2 garlic cloves, minced
3 tablespoons canola oil
2-1/2 pounds fresh broccoli, cut into florets (about 10 cups)
1/4 cup chicken broth
1/2 teaspoon dried oregano
1/2 teaspoon salt
1/8 teaspoon pepper
2 tablespoons sunflower kernels

In a large skillet, saute garlic in oil for 1 minute. Add broccoli; cook and stir for 3 minutes.

Add the chicken broth, oregano, salt and pepper; cover and cook until broccoli is crisp-tender, about 4 minutes. Sprinkle with sunflower kernels. **Yield:** 10 servings.

Nutritional Analysis: One serving (3/4 cup) equals 80 calories, 6 g fat (trace saturated fat), 0 cholesterol, 174 mg sodium, 7 g carbohydrate, 3 g fiber, 4 g protein. **Diabetic Exchanges:** 1 vegetable, 1 fat.

Peanut Butter Chocolate Cake

2-1/4 cups all-purpose flour
1-1/2 cups sugar
  1/3 cup baking cocoa
1-1/2 teaspoons baking soda
  1/2 teaspoon salt
1-1/2 cups water
  1/2 cup vegetable oil
4-1/2 teaspoons white vinegar
1-1/2 teaspoons vanilla extract
PEANUT BUTTER BATTER:
    4 ounces cream cheese, softened
  1/4 cup creamy peanut butter
  1/3 cup plus 1 tablespoon sugar, *divided*
    1 egg
  1/8 teaspoon salt

  1/2 cup semisweet chocolate chips
  1/2 cup chopped pecans

In a large bowl, combine the flour, sugar, cocoa, baking soda and salt. Stir in water, oil, vinegar and vanilla; mix well. Pour into a greased 13-in. x 9-in. x 2-in. baking pan.

In a mixing bowl, beat cream cheese, peanut butter, 1/3 cup sugar, egg and salt until smooth. Stir in chocolate chips. Drop by tablespoonfuls over cake batter; cut through batter with a knife to swirl the peanut butter mixture. Sprinkle with pecans and remaining sugar.

Bake at 350° for 30-35 minutes or until a toothpick inserted near the center comes out clean. Cool on a wire rack before cutting. Refrigerate leftovers. **Yield:** 24 servings.

It's possible to save on your grocery bill without scrimping on flavor when feeding your family.

The recipes here are suggested by three budget-minded cooks and combined into a delicious meal you can serve for $1.43 per person.

Enchilada Casserole is a hearty, satisfying entree. Marcia Schmiedt of Anchorage, Alaska shares the zesty recipe.

Skillet Green Beans is a staple side dish in the Columbus, Michigan home of Linda Sugars.

June Brown of Veneta, Oregon recommends rich and smooth Frozen Chocolate Cream Pie.

Enchilada Casserole

     1 pound ground turkey
 1-1/2 cups chopped onions
     2 garlic cloves, minced
     1 tablespoon plus 1/3 cup vegetable oil, *divided*
   1/3 cup all-purpose flour
     2 tablespoons chili powder
   3/4 teaspoon seasoned salt
   1/8 teaspoon pepper
     4 cups water
    12 corn tortillas (7 inches)
 1-1/2 cups shredded cheddar cheese
 1-1/2 cups salsa

In a skillet over medium heat, cook the turkey, onions and garlic in 1 tablespoon oil until no longer pink; drain. Sprinkle with flour, chili powder, seasoned salt and pepper. Add water and bring to a boil. Reduce heat; simmer, uncovered, for 8-10 minutes or until reduced.

In another skillet, fry tortillas in remaining oil for about 15 seconds, turning once. Drain well. Cut nine tortillas in half. Place cut edge of one tortilla against each short side of a greased 11-in. x 7-in. x 2-in. baking dish. Place cut edge of two tortillas against long sides of dish, overlapping to fit. Place a whole tortilla in center.

Spoon 2 cups of meat mixture over tortillas; sprinkle with 1/2 cup cheese. Repeat layers. Top with remaining tortillas and sauce. Bake, uncovered, at 375° for 20 minutes. Sprinkle with remaining cheese. Bake 5-10 minutes longer or until cheese melts. Serve with salsa. **Yield:** 8 servings.

Skillet Green Beans

     1 medium onion, diced
   1/4 cup stick margarine
     2 packages (16 ounces *each*) frozen cut green beans, thawed
   1/4 teaspoon salt
   1/4 teaspoon pepper
   1/2 cup sour cream
Paprika, optional

In a skillet, saute onion in margarine until tender. Add beans, salt and pepper. Cook until heated through. Serve with sour cream; sprinkle with paprika if desired. **Yield:** 8 servings.

Frozen Chocolate Cream Pie

 1-1/2 cups graham cracker crumbs
     5 tablespoons sugar, *divided*
   1/3 cup stick margarine, melted
   1/2 cup plus 4 teaspoons semisweet chocolate chips, *divided*
     5 tablespoons milk, *divided*
     1 package (3 ounces) cream cheese, softened
 3-1/2 cups whipped topping, *divided*

In a bowl, combine the graham cracker crumbs and 3 tablespoons of sugar. Stir in the melted margarine. Press onto the bottom and up the sides of an ungreased 9-in. pie plate. Refrigerate the crust for 30 minutes.

In a microwave-safe bowl, combine 1/2 cup chocolate chips and 2 tablespoons milk. Microwave, uncovered, on high for 1-2 minutes or until melted. Stir to blend; set aside.

In another bowl, beat cream cheese and remaining sugar. Stir in chocolate mixture and remaining milk; beat until smooth. Set aside 1/2 cup whipped topping. Fold remaining whipped topping into chocolate mixture.

Spoon into crust. Freeze 4 hours or until firm. Garnish with the remaining whipped topping and chocolate chips **Yield:** 8 servings.

Tried Tortillas?

Packaged tortillas are available in the refrigerated section of most supermarkets across the country in a variety of forms.

Corn tortillas are made from corn flour; flour tortillas are made with all-purpose or whole wheat flour.

Tortillas and tortilla chips are the fastest-growing segment of the baked-goods industry. People in the U.S. now consume more tortillas than they do bagels, English muffins and pitas combined.

Does going out for Italian food feel like you've spent enough money to visit that country in person? Then feast your eyes on this mouth-watering meal and travel no further than your kitchen.

Three terrific cooks share the good-as-a-restaurant dishes, which add up to a mere $1.30 per plate!

Tomatoes, ground beef and mozzarella cheese flavor Aunt May's Lasagna. "Some people don't like the taste of ricotta cheese, which is traditionally found in lasagna. This recipe is a nice alternative," says Angie Estes of Elko, Nevada. "Pitted ripe olives are a delicious addition."

Garlic Tomato Bruschetta, from Jean Franzoni of Rutland, Vermont, makes a crispy complement to any Italian entree. "I started with my grandmother's recipe and just added fresh tomatoes," Jean explains.

"Walnut Romaine Salad offers plenty of crunch," notes Harriet Stichter of Milford, Indiana, "and a zippy vinegar and oil dressing."

$1.30 Per Serving

Aunt May's Lasagna

    1 pound ground beef
    1 large onion, chopped
    2 garlic cloves, minced
    1 can (28 ounces) stewed tomatoes
    2 cans (6 ounces *each*) tomato paste
    1 teaspoon dried basil
1/2 teaspoon dried oregano
1/4 teaspoon pepper
    1 bay leaf
    9 lasagna noodles
    1 can (6 ounces) pitted ripe olives,
       drained and coarsely chopped
    2 cups (8 ounces) shredded mozzarella
       cheese
1/2 cup grated Parmesan cheese

In a large saucepan, cook beef, onion and garlic over medium heat until meat is no longer pink; drain. Stir in the tomatoes, tomato paste, basil, oregano, pepper and bay leaf. Bring to a boil. Reduce heat; cover and simmer for 40-50 minutes or until thickened.

Meanwhile, cook noodles according to package directions; drain. Discard bay leaf from meat sauce. Stir in olives.

Spread a fourth of the meat sauce in a greased 13-in. x 9-in. x 2-in. baking dish. Top with three noodles and a third of the mozzarella and Parmesan cheeses. Repeat the layers. Top with the remaining noodles, meat sauce, mozzarella and Parmesan cheeses.

Bake, uncovered, at 350° for 35-40 minutes or until bubbly. Let stand for 15 minutes before cutting. **Yield:** 12 servings.

Garlic Tomato Bruschetta

✓ Uses less fat, sugar or salt. Includes Nutritional Analysis and Diabetic Exchanges.

1/4 cup olive oil
    3 tablespoons chopped fresh basil
    3 to 4 garlic cloves, minced
1/2 teaspoon salt
1/4 teaspoon pepper
    4 medium tomatoes, diced
    2 tablespoons grated Parmesan cheese
    1 loaf (1 pound) unsliced French
       bread

In a bowl, combine oil, basil, garlic, salt and pepper. Add tomatoes and toss gently. Sprinkle with

cheese. Refrigerate for at least 1 hour. Bring to room temperature before serving. Cut bread into 24 slices; toast under broiler until lightly browned. Top with tomato mixture. Serve immediately. **Yield:** 12 servings.

Nutritional Analysis: One serving (2 pieces) equals 156 calories, 6 g fat (1 g saturated fat), 1 mg cholesterol, 347 mg sodium, 22 g carbohydrate, 1 g fiber, 4 g protein. **Diabetic Exchanges:** 1 starch, 1 vegetable, 1 fat.

Walnut Romaine Salad

1 small bunch romaine, torn
1 small zucchini, chopped
1 cup seasoned salad croutons
1/4 cup chopped walnuts
2 tablespoons red wine vinegar
2 tablespoons Dijon mustard
2 tablespoons honey
1 garlic clove, minced
Dash pepper
6 tablespoons olive oil

In a large bowl, toss the romaine, zucchini, croutons and walnuts.

In a small bowl, whisk the vinegar, Dijon mustard, honey, garlic and pepper until smooth. Slowly whisk in the olive oil. Serve dressing with the salad. Refrigerate any leftover dressing. **Yield:** 12 servings.

Dishing out hearty helpings of down-home foods to your family doesn't mean you also have to fork out tons of money.

Three frugal cooks prove it with this delicious fare perfect for a Sunday dinner. Our Test Kitchen staff estimates the cost at just $1.64 per setting.

"Country Roasted Chicken gets wonderful flavor from the celery, onion and parsley tucked inside," says Judy Page of Edenville, Michigan. "This is my family's favorite way to eat poultry. When my daughter was away at school, she even called home to ask me for a copy of the recipe so she could make it herself."

Dot's Corn Muffins are from Dorothy Smith, an El Dorado, Arkansas cook. "Moist and golden, these muffins are quick to make and go well with almost any meal," she says. "They're especially good with a hot bowl of soup."

"Creamed Carrots are always popular at my table," declares Eva Bailey of Olive Hill, Kentucky. "The rich sauce coats the carrots nicely and really perks up their flavor."

Country Roasted Chicken

  1 broiler/fryer chicken (3 pounds)
1/2 teaspoon dried thyme
  2 teaspoons salt, *divided*
  1 large onion, cut into eighths
  2 celery ribs with leaves, cut into 4-inch
     pieces
  4 fresh parsley sprigs
  8 small red potatoes
1/4 cup chicken broth
1/4 cup minced fresh parsley

Sprinkle inside of chicken with thyme and 1 teaspoon salt. Stuff with onion, celery and parsley sprigs. Place in a greased Dutch oven. Cover and bake at 375° for 30 minutes. Sprinkle remaining salt over chicken. Add potatoes and broth to pan. Cover and bake 25 minutes longer.

Increase oven temperature to 400°. Bake, uncovered, for 10-15 minutes or until potatoes are tender and a meat thermometer inserted in the chicken thighs reads 180°. Sprinkle with minced parsley. **Yield:** 4 servings.

Dot's Corn Muffins

1/2 cup all-purpose flour
1/2 cup cornmeal
  3 tablespoons sugar
1/2 teaspoon baking soda
1/2 teaspoon salt
  1 egg
  1 cup (8 ounces) sour cream

$1.64 Per Person

In a bowl, combine the flour, cornmeal, sugar, baking soda and salt. In another bowl, beat egg and sour cream; stir into dry ingredients just until moistened. Fill greased muffin cups two-thirds full.

Bake at 400° for 15-18 minutes or until a toothpick inserted near the middle comes out clean. Cool for 5 minutes before removing from pan to a wire rack. **Yield:** 8 muffins.

Creamed Carrots

1 pound carrots, sliced
1 tablespoon butter
1 tablespoon all-purpose flour

2 tablespoons finely chopped onion
2 teaspoons chopped fresh basil
1/2 teaspoon seasoned salt
1/8 teaspoon pepper
1 cup evaporated milk

In a large saucepan, bring 1 in. of water and carrots to a boil. Reduce heat; cover and simmer for 7-9 minutes or until crisp-tender.

Meanwhile, in another saucepan, melt butter. Stir in flour, onion, basil, seasoned salt and pepper until blended. Gradually stir in milk. Bring to a boil; cook and stir for 2 minutes or until thickened. Drain carrots; place in a serving bowl. Add sauce and stir to coat. **Yield:** 4 servings.

Keeping Carrots

Carrots were originally red, purple or black until the early 17th century, when the orange variety was developed in Holland.

Remove the green leafy tops from the carrots before they are stored. Otherwise, the tops will draw moisture from the carrots, cause them to become bitter and reduce their storage life. Carrots should be stored in sealed plastic bags in the refrigerator.

You can save on your grocery bill without scrimping on flavor when feeding your family…this nicely seasoned Mexican meal proves it!

Our Test Kitchen home economists have combined the three recipes here into a delicious and satisfying meal you can put on the table for just $1.72 per person.

The hearty Turkey Enchiladas are generously stuffed with cubed turkey, cheese and chilies in a mild creamy sauce. "My daughter made this dish for us, and it was excellent," raves Leona Therou of Overland Park, Kansas.

Sweet Pepper Salad, from Lu Ann Kessi of Eddyville, Oregon, is crisp and colorful with a tangy dressing. It's a wonderful alternative to the regular tossed green salad.

Light and spongy Chiffon Cake makes a fitting finale to any meal. Arlene Murphy of Beverly Hills, Florida shares the delicious recipe.

$1.72 Per Serving

Turkey Enchiladas

1 medium onion, chopped
1/3 cup chopped green pepper
2 tablespoons vegetable oil
2 cups cubed cooked turkey
1 cup (4 ounces) shredded
   Colby-Monterey Jack cheese,
   divided
1 can (4 ounces) chopped green chilies
1 cup (8 ounces) sour cream
1 can (10-3/4 ounces) condensed cream
   of chicken soup, undiluted
1/4 teaspoon ground coriander
1/8 teaspoon ground cumin
6 flour tortillas (8 inches), warmed

In a large skillet, saute the onion and green pepper in oil until vegetables are tender; remove from the heat. Stir in the turkey, 1/2 cup of cheese and green chilies; set aside. In a saucepan, combine the sour cream, soup, coriander and cumin. Cook and stir over low heat until warm; stir 1/2 cup into the turkey mixture.

Spoon about 1/3 cup turkey filling down the center of each tortilla and roll up tightly. Place tortillas seam side down in a greased 13-in. x 9-in. x 2-in. baking dish.

Spoon the remaining soup mixture down the center of the tortillas. Sprinkle with remaining cheese. Bake, uncovered, at 350° for 20-25 minutes or until heated through. **Yield:** 6 servings.

Sweet Pepper Salad

3 medium green peppers, thinly sliced
1 medium sweet red pepper, thinly sliced
1 medium red onion, thinly sliced
1 teaspoon grated lemon peel
1/2 cup red wine vinegar
4-1/2 teaspoons vegetable oil
1 tablespoon minced fresh basil
1 tablespoon sugar
1/4 teaspoon salt
1/8 teaspoon pepper

In a salad bowl, combine the peppers, onion and lemon peel. Combine vinegar and oil; pour over vegetables and toss to coat. Cover and refrigerate overnight.

Just before serving, add the basil, sugar, salt and pepper; mix well. **Yield:** 6 servings.

Chiffon Cake

6 eggs, *separated*
1/2 teaspoon salt
1-1/2 cups sugar, *divided*
1/2 cup warm water
1-1/2 cups all-purpose flour, *divided*
1 teaspoon vanilla extract
1/2 teaspoon cream of tartar
1/2 cup chocolate ice cream topping

In a mixing bowl, beat the egg yolks and salt for 2 minutes. Gradually beat in 1 cup sugar; beat 2 minutes longer. Gradually add the water; beat about 2-1/2 minutes longer or until frothy. Beat in 3/4 cup flour. Beat in vanilla extract and all of the remaining flour.

In another mixing bowl, beat the egg whites until foamy. Add cream of tartar; beat until soft peaks form. Gradually beat in remaining sugar, 1 tablespoon at a time, on high until stiff peaks form. Fold into egg yolk mixture.

Transfer to an ungreased 10-in. tube pan. Bake at 325° for 55-60 minutes or until top springs back when lightly touched and cracks feel dry. Immediately invert pan onto a wire rack; cool completely.

Run a knife around the sides of the pan to remove the cake. Slice and drizzle with ice cream topping. **Yield:** 12 servings.

Even when your grocery budget is tight, you can still enjoy foods with full flavor and leave the table satisfied.

Three frugal cooks prove it with this company-quality meal. Our Test Kitchen home economists estimate the cost at $1.61 per setting.

"Creamy Baked Chicken is comforting and easy to prepare," says Barbara Clarke of Punta Gorda, Florida. "It's great to serve guests."

Broccoli with Almonds is a tasty, dressed-up side dish from Verna Puntigan of Pasadena, Maryland.

Deborah Sheehan of East Orland, Maine says Chocolate Oatmeal Cake is a treat. "It's so moist, plus it's topped with scrumptious coffee frosting."

$1.61 Per Person

Creamy Baked Chicken

1 broiler/fryer chicken (3 pounds), cut up
1 can (10-3/4 ounces) condensed cream of chicken soup, undiluted
1 can (10-3/4 ounces) condensed cream of mushroom soup, undiluted
1 cup (8 ounces) sour cream
1/2 cup water
1 teaspoon minced chives
Salt and pepper to taste
1/2 teaspoon paprika

Place chicken in a greased 13-in. x 9-in. x 2-in. baking dish. In a bowl, combine the soups, sour cream, water, chives, salt and pepper; spoon over chicken. Sprinkle with paprika. Bake, uncovered, at 350° for 1 hour or until chicken juices run clear. **Yield:** 6 servings.

Broccoli with Almonds

1-1/2 pounds fresh broccoli, cut into spears
1 cup water
1 teaspoon chicken bouillon granules
1/4 cup sliced almonds
3 tablespoons stick margarine
1/2 cup finely chopped onion
1 teaspoon salt

In a large saucepan, bring the broccoli, water and bouillon to a boil. Reduce heat; cover and simmer for 5-8 minutes or until broccoli is crisp-tender. Drain and place in a serving dish; keep warm.

In a skillet, saute the almonds in margarine until browned. Add the onion and salt; saute until onion is tender. Pour over broccoli; toss to coat. **Yield:** 6 servings.

Chocolate Oatmeal Cake

1-1/2 cups boiling water
1 cup quick-cooking oats

1 cup (6 ounces) semisweet chocolate chips
1/2 cup stick margarine, softened
3/4 cup sugar
3/4 cup packed brown sugar
2 eggs
1-1/2 cups all-purpose flour
1 teaspoon baking soda
1 teaspoon salt
COFFEE FROSTING:
2 teaspoons instant coffee granules
1/4 cup half-and-half cream, warmed
1/2 cup stick margarine, softened
1 teaspoon vanilla extract
1/8 teaspoon salt
4 cups confectioners' sugar

In a bowl, combine the water and oats. Sprinkle with chocolate chips (do not stir); let stand for 20 minutes. In a mixing bowl, cream margarine and sugars. Add eggs, one at a time, beating well after each addition. Beat in oat mixture. Combine flour, baking soda and salt; add to the creamed mixture and mix well.

Pour into a greased 13-in. x 9-in. x 2-in. baking pan. Bake at 350° for 35-40 minutes or until a toothpick inserted near the center comes out clean. Cool on a wire rack.

For frosting, dissolve coffee granules in cream; set aside. In a small mixing bowl, cream margarine; add vanilla and salt. Slowly beat in sugar. Beat in enough of coffee mixture to achieve spreading consistency. Frost the cake. **Yield:** 12 servings.

Broccoli Basics

Broccoli is available year-round, but it is best from October through May. Buy broccoli with a deep, strong color—green, or green tinged with purple. The buds should be tightly closed and the leaves crisp.

Turn leftover broccoli into a delicious bisque. Simply put it into a blender, and add milk, broth or cream, and a shot of sherry or cooking sherry. Then process until smooth. Strain if desired and heat gently or serve cold.

Come the cooler fall months, country cooks head to the kitchen to prepare hearty down-home fare for their families.

You can be frugal and still prepare a full-flavored dinner—three budget-conscious cooks prove it with this trio of home-style recipes. Our Test Kitchen staff estimates the total cost for this meal at just $1.51 per serving!

Pineapple Ham Loaf is a satisfying and inexpensive main dish. "This loaf is nice enough for the holidays, but we have it often for everyday meals, too, since it's so easy to prepare and easy on the pocketbook," shares Linda Manley of Morgantown, West Virginia.

Broccoli Cream Soup has a wonderful fresh flavor. "I've never had a better broccoli soup," says Beth Hart of Walworth, New York. "It warms you all over."

And you don't have to break the bank to enjoy a batch of golden dinner rolls. Buttermilk Rolls, from Bernice Morris of Marshfield, Missouri, are a real treat served alongside any entree.

$1.51 Per Serving

Pineapple Ham Loaf

    2 eggs
    1 cup milk
    1 cup crushed saltines (about 30
      crackers)
    1/2 teaspoon salt
    1/8 teaspoon pepper
1-1/2 pounds ground fully cooked ham
    1/2 pound ground pork
    1/4 cup packed brown sugar
      2 tablespoons cider vinegar
      1 teaspoon ground mustard
      1 can (8 ounces) sliced pineapple,
        drained

In a large bowl, combine the first five ingredients. Crumble ham and pork over mixture; mix well. Combine the brown sugar, vinegar and mustard; pour into an ungreased 9-in. x 5-in. x 3-in. loaf pan. Arrange three pineapple slices in pan (refrigerate remaining pineapple for another use). Pat meat mixture into pan.

Cover and bake at 325° for 1-1/2 hours. Uncover; bake 30 minutes longer or until meat a thermometer reads 160°. Let stand for 15 minutes. Invert onto a serving platter. **Yield:** 8 servings.

Broccoli Cream Soup

    9 cups fresh broccoli florets
    4 cups chicken broth
    1 medium onion, chopped
    8 tablespoons butter, *divided*
    1 bay leaf
    3/4 teaspoon *each* salt and white pepper
    1/4 teaspoon *each* onion salt and garlic
      salt
Pinch *each* dried basil, thyme and rubbed
    sage
Dash hot pepper sauce
    7 tablespoons all-purpose flour
    2 cups milk
    1 cup buttermilk
    1/2 cup heavy whipping cream

In a large saucepan, bring broccoli and broth to a boil. Reduce heat; simmer for 5 minutes. In a small skillet, saute onion in 2 tablespoons butter until tender; add to broccoli mixture. Stir in the bay leaf and remaining seasonings. Simmer, uncovered, for 5 minutes.

In a small saucepan, melt the remaining butter.

Stir in flour until smooth. Gradually add milk. Bring to a boil; cook and stir for 2 minutes or until thickened. Stir into broccoli mixture; add buttermilk and cream. Heat through (do not boil). Discard bay leaf. **Yield:** 8 servings (about 2 quarts).

Buttermilk Rolls

    1 package (1/4 ounce) active dry yeast
  1/4 cup warm water (110° to 115°)
1-1/2 cups warm buttermilk (110° to 115°)
  1/2 cup vegetable oil
    3 tablespoons sugar
    1 teaspoon salt
  1/2 teaspoon baking soda
4-1/2 cups all-purpose flour

In a mixing bowl, dissolve yeast in water. Beat in the buttermilk, oil, sugar, salt, baking soda and 2 cups flour until smooth. Stir in enough remaining flour to form a soft dough.

Turn onto a floured surface; knead until smooth and elastic, about 6-8 minutes. Place in a greased bowl, turning once to grease top. Cover and let rise in a warm place until doubled, about 1-1/2 hours.

Punch the dough down. Divide dough into 18 pieces and roll into balls. Place on greased baking sheets. Cover and let rise until doubled, about 30 minutes. Bake rolls at 400° for 15-20 minutes or until golden brown. Cool on wire racks. **Yield:** 1-1/2 dozen.

Editor's Note: Warmed buttermilk will appear curdled

If you're looking for a great supper or lunch that doesn't require loads of preparation time or lots of money, try this menu.

Our Test Kitchen staff combined dishes from three budget-conscious cooks to create this super spread. They estimate the total cost at just $1.62 per setting.

Hot Beef Cheddar Subs are like cheesy sloppy joes tucked into hollowed-out crusty rolls. "My family devours these yummy sandwiches," says Marann Reilly of Lithia Springs, Georgia, "so I like to serve them often."

Donna Cline of Pensacola, Florida frequently brightens her dinner table with a big bowl full of fresh veggies. "We especially enjoy Zucchini 'n' Carrot Coins in the summer, when garden-picked vegetables are plentiful and delicious," she says. "No one can resist this scrumptious vegetable side dish."

Fluffy Lemon Dessert is a fabulous finale from Linda Nilsen of Anoka, Minnesota. "Each May, I bring this refreshing, melt-in-your-mouth treat to our last church circle meeting of the year," she says. "It's economical and so well-received that I'm not sure they'd let me in without it! I'm always asked for copies of the recipe."

$1.62 Per Person

Hot Beef Cheddar Subs

>   4 submarine sandwich buns
>   1 pound ground beef
>   1 medium green pepper, diced
>   1 small onion, diced
>   1 can (10-3/4 ounces) condensed cheddar
>   cheese soup, undiluted
> 1/4 teaspoon Worcestershire sauce
>   4 slices American cheese

Cut a thin slice off top of each bun; set tops aside. Carefully hollow out bottoms, leaving a 1/2-in. shell. Set aside 1/2 cup bread.

In a skillet, cook beef, pepper and onion over medium heat until meat is no longer pink; drain. Stir in soup, Worcestershire sauce and reserved bread; mix well.

Spoon meat mixture into hollowed-out buns; top each with a cheese slice. Replace tops. Place on an ungreased baking sheet. Bake, uncovered, at 350° for 5-7 minutes or until cheese is melted. **Yield:** 4 servings.

Zucchini 'n' Carrot Coins

>   1 pound carrots, thinly sliced
>   2 tablespoons butter
>   1 small onion, sliced and separated into
>   rings
>   2 small zucchini, cut into 1/4-inch slices

>   2 teaspoons dried basil
> 1/2 teaspoon salt
> 1/4 teaspoon pepper

In a large skillet, saute sliced carrots in butter for 4-5 minutes. Add the onion; cook for 1 minute. Stir in the remaining ingredients. Cover and cook 4-5 minutes or until the vegetables are crisp-tender. **Yield:** 4 servings.

Fluffy Lemon Dessert

>   1 can (12 ounces) evaporated milk
>   1 package (3 ounces) lemon gelatin
>   1 cup sugar
> 1-3/4 cups boiling water
> 1/4 cup lemon juice

3/4 cup whipped topping
1 medium lemon, sliced
10 mint sprigs

Pour milk into a small mixing bowl; place the mixer beaters in the bowl. Cover and refrigerate for at least 2 hours or until chilled.

Meanwhile, in a large mixing bowl, dissolve gelatin and sugar in water. Stir in lemon juice. Cover and refrigerate until syrupy, about 1-1/2 hours.

Beat the gelatin until tiny bubbles form. Beat chilled milk until soft peaks form; fold into gelatin. Pour into serving dishes. Refrigerate for at least 3 hours or overnight.

Garnish servings with the whipped topping, lemon and mint. Refrigerate any leftovers. **Yield:** 10 servings.

Great Ground Beef

Ground beef is not only tasty and versatile...it also won't break your grocery budget. Perhaps that's why it's an indispensable ingredient in kitchens across the country.

It is often sold in large, economy sizes. These packages are a bargain because you can use some of the ground beef now and freeze some for another use.

Uncooked ground beef can be frozen for 2 weeks in its original packaging. Thaw ground beef only in the refrigerator or microwave; never thaw it at room temperature.

You can watch your money and still prepare a satisfying, full-flavored fall meal for your family. Three budget-conscious cooks prove it with these recipes. Our Test Kitchen staff estimates the cost for this meal at 99¢ a serving.

Hearty and wonderfully seasoned Bean Counter Chowder is suggested by Vivian Haen of Menomonee Falls, Wisconsin.

Soft Onion Breadsticks make a yummy, inexpensive addition to any meal. The recipe is from Maryellen Hays of Wolcottville, Indiana.

There's always room for dessert—and there's sure to be room in your budget, too—for Strawberry Sandwich Cookies. "They're crisp and fruity and very pretty," shares Barbara Sessoyeff of Redwood Valley, California.

99¢ Per Serving

Bean Counter Chowder

✓ Uses less fat, sugar or salt. Includes Nutritional Analysis and Diabetic Exchanges.

     1/2 cup chopped onion
       2 garlic cloves, minced
       1 tablespoon vegetable oil
       1 medium tomato, chopped
       2 cans (14-1/2 ounces *each*) chicken broth
1-3/4 cups water
     1/2 teaspoon *each* dried basil, oregano and
           celery flakes
     1/4 teaspoon pepper
       3 cans (15-1/4 ounces *each*) great
           northern *or* pinto beans, rinsed and
           drained
       1 cup uncooked elbow macaroni
       1 tablespoon minced fresh parsley

In a large saucepan, saute onion and garlic in oil until tender. Add tomato; simmer for 5 minutes. Add the broth, water and seasonings. Bring to a boil; cook for 5 minutes. Add beans and macaroni; return to a boil. Reduce heat; simmer, uncovered, for 15 minutes or until macaroni is tender. Sprinkle with parsley. **Yield:** 8 servings (2 quarts).

Nutritional Analysis: One serving (1 cup) equals 285 calories, 3 g fat (1 g saturated fat), 0 cholesterol, 447 mg sodium, 48 g carbohydrate, 9 g fiber, 17 g protein. **Diabetic Exchanges:** 3 starch, 1 meat.

Soft Onion Breadsticks

     3/4 cup chopped onion
       1 tablespoon vegetable oil
       1 package (1/4 ounce) active dry yeast
     1/2 cup warm water (110° to 115°)
     1/2 cup warm milk (110° to 115°)
       2 eggs
     1/4 cup butter, softened

       1 tablespoon sugar
1-1/2 teaspoons salt
3-1/2 to 4 cups all-purpose flour
       2 tablespoons cold water
       2 tablespoons sesame seeds
       1 tablespoon poppy seeds

In a skillet, saute onion in oil until tender; cool. In a mixing bowl, dissolve yeast in warm water. Add milk, 1 egg, butter, sugar, salt and 1 cup flour. Beat on medium speed for 2 minutes. Stir in the onion and enough remaining flour to form a soft dough. Turn onto a floured surface; knead until smooth and elastic, about 6-8 minutes. Place in a greased bowl, turning once to grease top. Cover and let rise until doubled, about 1 hour.

Punch dough down. Let stand for 10 minutes. Turn onto a lightly floured surface; divide into 32 pieces. Shape each piece into an 8-in. rope. Place 2 in. apart on greased baking sheets. Cover and let

rise in a warm place for 15 minutes.

Beat cold water and remaining egg; brush over breadsticks. Sprinkle half with sesame seeds and half with poppy seeds. Bake at 350° for 16-22 minutes or until golden brown. Remove to wire racks. **Yield:** 32 breadsticks.

Strawberry Sandwich Cookies

1 cup blanched almonds
3/4 cup stick margarine, softened
1 cup confectioners' sugar, *divided*
1 egg
1/2 teaspoon almond extract
1-1/2 cups all-purpose flour
1/8 teaspoon salt
1 tablespoon lemon juice
3 tablespoons strawberry preserves

In a food processor or blender, process almonds until ground; set aside. In a mixing bowl, cream margarine and 1/2 cup sugar. Beat in egg and extract. Combine flour and salt; gradually add to creamed mixture. Stir in the ground almonds. Divide dough in half; cover and refrigerate for 2 hours or until easy to handle.

On a lightly floured surface, roll out each portion of dough into a 12-in. x 9-in. rectangle. Cut lengthwise into three strips; cut each strip widthwise into six pieces. With a 3/4-in. round cutter, cut out a circle in the center of half of the pieces (discard circles). Place 1 in. apart on ungreased baking sheets. Bake at 375° for 8-10 minutes or until golden brown. Remove to wire racks to cool.

For glaze, combine lemon juice and remaining sugar; thinly spread over whole cookies. Top with cutout cookies; fill center with 1/2 teaspoon preserves. **Yield:** 1-1/2 dozen.

Hearty and filling, casseroles are a good choice when you're trying to keep your grocery bills in check and still provide your family with a pleasing, tasty dinner.

The complete meal here is inexpensive yet delicious. Three good cooks recommend these delightful dishes, and our Test Kitchen staff estimates the total cost at a mere $1.69 per setting.

Pork Noodle Casserole is a savory entree suggested by Bernice Morris of Marshfield, Missouri. "One of the less expensive cuts of pork becomes tender and tasty in this creamy meal-in-one casserole," Bernice notes.

In Buckley, Washington, Betty Brown's family enjoys Beans with Cherry Tomatoes. "We love this dressed-up version of garden green beans," Betty says. "This skillet side dish goes great with any meat entree."

Delicious Pretzel Dessert saves both time and money. "The recipe makes a big batch of this sweet and salty, creamy and crunchy treat," says Rita Winterberger from her home in Huson, Montana.

"That's fine with us," says Rita," because any dessert that's left over is super the next day, too."

$1.69 Per Person

Pork Noodle Casserole

   2 cups uncooked egg noodles
   2 pounds boneless pork, cut into 3/4-inch cubes
   2 medium onions, chopped
   2 cans (15-1/4 ounces *each*) whole kernel corn, drained
   2 cans (10-3/4 ounces *each*) condensed cream of mushroom soup, undiluted
   1/2 teaspoon salt
   1/2 teaspoon pepper

Cook noodles according to package directions. In a large skillet, cook pork and onions over medium heat until meat is no longer pink. Drain noodles. Stir noodles, corn, soup, salt and pepper into pork mixture.

Transfer to a greased 3-qt. baking dish. Cover and bake at 350° for 30 minutes. Uncover; bake 15 minutes longer. **Yield:** 8 servings.

Beans with Cherry Tomatoes

   4 bacon strips, diced
1-1/2 pounds fresh green beans, cut into 2-inch pieces
   4 garlic cloves, thinly sliced
1-1/2 cups halved cherry tomatoes
   1/2 teaspoon salt
   1/4 cup slivered almonds, toasted

In a large skillet, cook the bacon over medium heat until crisp. Remove bacon to paper towels to drain. In the drippings, saute the beans for 12-14 minutes or until crisp-tender. Add the garlic and cook 2-3 minutes longer. Stir in the tomatoes and salt; heat through. Sprinkle with bacon and almonds. **Yield:** 8 servings.

Pretzel Dessert

   2 cups crushed pretzels
   3/4 cup sugar
   3/4 cup stick margarine, melted
   2 envelopes whipped topping mix
   1 cup cold milk
   1 teaspoon vanilla extract

1 package (8 ounces) cream cheese, cubed
1 cup confectioners' sugar
1 can (21 ounces) cherry pie filling

In a bowl, combine the pretzels, sugar and margarine; set aside 1/2 cup for topping. Press the remaining mixture into an ungreased 13-in. x 9-in. x 2-in. dish.

In a mixing bowl, beat whipped topping mix, milk and vanilla on high speed for 4 minutes or until soft peaks form. Add cream cheese and confectioners' sugar; beat until smooth.

Spread half over crust. Top with the pie filling and remaining cream cheese mixture. Sprinkle with reserved pretzel mixture. Refrigerate overnight. **Yield:** 16 servings.

Picking Green Beans

Green beans are also called string beans and snap beans; the yellow variety is known as wax beans.

Select fresh beans that have firm, smooth and brightly colored pods. They should be crisp enough to snap when bent in half. Avoid those that look discolored, spotted or leathery.

Be careful not to overcook fresh beans—they should be crisp-tender when done. Overdone beans will lose some of their bright color as well as their fresh flavor.

You don't hear the slogan "change back from your dollar" anymore at restaurants, but you can still feed your family at home for under a buck a plate. This well-rounded meal is tasty, wholesome and much more satisfying than fast food.

The menu was compiled from three great cooks who each shared one of their family's favorite recipes. The result is a meal that costs just 94¢ per serving.

Brisket for a Bunch makes tender slices of beef in a delicious au jus. Dawn Fagerstrom of Warren, Minnesota suggests the recipe. To easily get very thin slices, chill the brisket before slicing, then reheat in the juices.

Cabbage Tossed Salad is a fun and interesting cross between a green salad and a coleslaw with a tangy dressing. The recipe is recommended by Marilyn Katcsmorak from Pleasanton, Texas.

The recipe for Apple Fritter Rings is an old-fashioned treat that comes from Bernice Snowberger of Monticello, Indiana.

94¢ Per Serving

Brisket for a Bunch

   1 beef brisket (2-1/2 pounds), cut in half
   1 tablespoon vegetable oil
1/2 cup chopped celery
1/2 cup chopped onion
3/4 cup beef broth
1/2 cup tomato sauce
1/4 cup water
1/4 cup sugar
   2 tablespoons onion soup mix
   1 tablespoon vinegar
12 hamburger buns, split

In a large skillet, brown the brisket on all sides in oil; transfer to a slow cooker. In the same skillet, saute celery and onion for 1 minute. Gradually add broth, tomato sauce and water; stir to loosen the browned bits from pan. Add sugar, soup mix and vinegar; bring to a boil. Pour over brisket.

Cover and cook on low for 7-8 hours or until meat is tender. Let stand for 5 minutes before slicing. Skim fat from cooking juices. Serve meat in buns with cooking juices. **Yield:** 12 servings.

Editor's Note: This recipe is for fresh beef brisket, not corned beef.

Cabbage Tossed Salad

✓ Uses less fat, sugar or salt. Includes Nutritional Analysis and Diabetic Exchanges.

5 cups chopped iceberg lettuce
2 cups chopped cabbage
2 cups chopped red cabbage
2 celery ribs, chopped
3 green onions with tops, sliced
1/2 cup vinegar

1/4 cup vegetable oil
4-1/2 teaspoons sugar
3/4 teaspoon salt, optional
1/4 teaspoon pepper
1/4 teaspoon garlic powder

In a large bowl, toss the lettuce, cabbage, celery and onions. In a small bowl, whisk together the remaining ingredients. Pour over salad and toss to coat. Chill for 30 minutes. **Yield:** 12 servings.

Nutritional Analysis: One serving (prepared with sugar substitute equivalent to 4-1/2 teaspoons sugar and without salt) equals 54 calories, 14 mg sodium, 0 cholesterol, 3 g carbohydrate, 1 g protein, 5 g fat, 1 g fiber. **Diabetic Exchanges:** 1 fat, 1/2 vegetable.

Apple Fritter Rings

1 egg
2/3 cup milk
1 teaspoon vegetable oil
1 cup all-purpose flour
2 tablespoons sugar
1 teaspoon baking powder
Dash salt
5 large tart apples
1-1/2 cups vegetable oil
1/4 cup sugar
1/2 teaspoon ground cinnamon

In a bowl, beat egg, milk and oil. Combine flour, sugar, baking powder and salt; stir into egg mixture until smooth (batter will be thick). Peel, core and cut apples into 1/2-in. rings. In an electric skillet or deep-fat fryer, heat oil to 375°. Dip rings into batter; fry, a few at a time, until golden. Drain on paper towels. Combine sugar and cinnamon; sprinkle over hot fritters. Serve warm. **Yield:** about 2 dozen.

Fryer Facts
The pot in which you deep-fry should be filled no more than halfway with oil. It's best to fry food in small batches.

Even at today's prices, you and your family can eat well without spending a king's ransom.

With its vibrant colors and tasty sauces, this dinner looks rich. The fact that it wasn't expensive can be your little secret. Three great cooks created the meal, and our Test Kitchen staff estimates the total cost at just $1.59 per setting.

Applesauce Pork Chops, from Elaine Anderson of Aliquippa, Pennsylvania, are fast, easy and delicious.

Sunny Carrot Sticks have a lightly sweet sauce with a delicate orange flavor. The recipe comes from Wendy Masters of Grand Valley, Ontario.

Glazed Butter Cookies are suggested by Dorothy Jennings of Waterloo, Iowa, who notes they aren't just for Christmastime. "I bake these cookies all year, changing cookie cutters for various occasions," says Dorothy.

Applesauce Pork Chops

    4 rib pork chops (1/2 inch thick)
    2 tablespoons vegetable oil
    1 large red apple
1-1/2 cups applesauce
    1 cup water
  1/4 cup chopped onion
    1 tablespoon Worcestershire sauce
  1/2 teaspoon garlic powder
  1/2 teaspoon salt
  1/4 teaspoon pepper
    1 package (6 ounces) chicken-flavored
      wild rice mix
    2 teaspoons cornstarch
    1 tablespoon cold water

In a skillet over medium-high heat, brown the pork chops in oil on both sides; drain. Cut four thin wedges from the apple; set aside. Peel and chop the remaining apple. Add chopped apple, applesauce, water, onion, Worcestershire sauce, garlic powder, salt and pepper to the skillet. Cover and simmer for 30-35 minutes or until the meat juices run clear.

Meanwhile, prepare rice according to package directions. Remove pork chops and keep warm. Combine cornstarch and cold water until smooth; stir into apple mixture. Bring to a boil; cook and stir for 2 minutes. Return chops to skillet and heat through. Serve with rice. Garnish with reserved apple wedges. **Yield:** 4 servings.

Sunny Carrot Sticks

    1 pound carrots, julienned
    1 tablespoon brown sugar
    1 teaspoon cornstarch
  1/4 cup orange juice
    2 tablespoons butter

$1.59 Per Person

Place carrots and a small amount of water in a saucepan; cover and cook until tender. Meanwhile, in another saucepan, combine brown sugar and cornstarch. Stir in orange juice until smooth.

Bring to a boil; cook and stir for 2 minutes or until thickened and bubbly. Stir in butter. Drain carrots; top with orange juice mixture and toss to coat. **Yield:** 4 servings.

Glazed Butter Cookies

  1/2 cup butter, softened
  3/4 cup sugar
    1 egg
  3/4 teaspoon vanilla extract
1-3/4 cups all-purpose flour

1/2 teaspoon baking powder
1/4 teaspoon salt
GLAZE:
   1 cup confectioners' sugar
   1 to 2 tablespoons milk
Red, green and yellow liquid *or* paste food coloring

In a mixing bowl, cream butter and sugar. Beat in egg and vanilla. Combine dry ingredients; gradually add to the creamed mixture. Cover and chill for 1 hour or until easy to handle.

On a lightly floured surface, roll out to 1/8-in. thickness. Cut with 2-1/2-in. cookie cutters. Place 1 in. apart on ungreased baking sheets. Bake at 350° for 8-10 minutes or until lightly browned. Cool on wire racks. In a small bowl, combine confectioners' sugar and enough milk until smooth. Stir in food coloring. Lightly spread onto cooled cookies. Let stand until glaze is set. **Yield:** 3 dozen.

Rolling Dough

Dust the rolling pin and surface lightly with flour to prevent dough from sticking. Roll out a portion of the cookie dough at a time. Keep the remaining dough in the refrigerator.

Roll dough to the recommended thickness. Be sure to roll evenly so each batch is of uniform thickness.

If you're looking for comfort food that won't put an uncomfortable crunch in your pocketbook, here's the menu for you.

This meat-and-potatoes meal comes from three experienced cooks who know what their families like…and you will like that it costs only $1.40 per setting.

Seasoned Swiss Steak combines tender beef and vegetables in a gravy that melds tomato, brown sugar and mustard. The recipe comes from Edna Hoffman of Hebron, Indiana.

Golden caramelized onions add a rich taste to Onion Mashed Potatoes, says Darlene Markel of Sublimity, Oregon. "We prefer them over plain mashed potatoes," says Darlene.

With her Apple-Berry Streusel Bars, Jane Acree of Holcomb, Illinois proves that inexpensive meals can include a scrumptious dessert. With fruity filling and nutty topping, these attractive bars taste like they cost a pretty penny!

$1.40 Per Serving

Seasoned Swiss Steak

1/4 cup all-purpose flour
1 tablespoon ground mustard
1 teaspoon salt, *divided*
1/4 teaspoon pepper, *divided*
1-1/2 pounds boneless round steak
(about 1 inch thick), cut into serving-size pieces
2 tablespoons vegetable oil
1 cup diced carrots
1/2 cup chopped onion
1/2 cup chopped green pepper
1 tablespoon brown sugar
1 tablespoon Worcestershire sauce
1 can (14-1/2 ounces) diced tomatoes, undrained
1/4 cup cold water

In a bowl, combine the flour, mustard, 1/2 teaspoon salt and 1/8 teaspoon pepper; set aside 2 tablespoons for gravy. Rub the remaining flour mixture over the steak. Pound steak with a meat mallet to tenderize.

In a skillet, brown steak in oil. Transfer to a greased 2-1/2-qt. baking dish. Top with carrots, onion, green pepper, brown sugar and Worcestershire sauce. Pour tomatoes over all. Cover and bake at 350° for 1-1/2 to 2 hours or until meat and vegetables are tender. Transfer meat and vegetables to a serving dish; keep warm.

Strain pan juices into a measuring cup; add water to measure 1 cup. In a saucepan, combine the reserved flour mixture with cold water until smooth. Whisk in the pan juices. Bring to a boil; cook and stir for 2 minutes or until thickened. Add the remaining salt and pepper. Serve gravy over the steak. **Yield:** 6 servings.

Onion Mashed Potatoes

4 medium potatoes, peeled and cubed
1 small onion, thinly sliced
1 teaspoon sugar
2 tablespoons butter
1/2 cup warm milk
1/2 teaspoon salt
1/8 teaspoon pepper
Minced fresh parsley, optional

Place potatoes in a saucepan and cover with water; bring to a boil. Cook until very tender, about 20-25 minutes. Meanwhile, in a skillet over low heat, cook onion and sugar in butter until golden, stirring frequently.

Drain and mash the potatoes. Add the milk, salt and pepper. Stir in the onion mixture. Garnish with parsley if desired. **Yield:** 6 servings.

Apple-Berry Streusel Bars

2-1/2 cups plus 2 tablespoons all-purpose
    flour, *divided*
    2 cups old-fashioned oats
1-1/4 cups sugar
    2 teaspoons baking powder
    1 teaspoon ground cinnamon
    1 cup butter, melted
    3 cups thinly sliced peeled tart apples
    1 jar (12 ounces) raspberry preserves
1/2 cup finely chopped walnuts

In a mixing bowl, combine 2-1/2 cups flour, oats, sugar, baking powder and cinnamon. Beat in butter just until moistened. Set aside 2 cups for topping. Pat remaining oat mixture into a greased 13-in. x 9-in. x 2-in. baking pan. Bake at 375° for 15 minutes. Meanwhile, toss apples with remaining flour.

Stir in the preserves; spread over hot crust to within 1/2 in. of edges. Combine nuts and reserved oat mixture; sprinkle over fruit mixture. Bake 30-35 minutes longer or until lightly browned. Cool completely before cutting. **Yield:** 4 dozen.

Fresh and Fruity

Jams and jellies can be produced from a number of artificial ingredients, so it's best to read the labels and purchase those made from real fruit. If they are and are labeled "light", so much the better —that's an indication that the sugar content has been reduced.

Are you looking to trim the amount of your family budget devoted to grocery shopping? This menu will help.

The frugal yet flavorful meal here is from three terrific cooks. The total cost is estimated at just $1.59 per setting.

This complete, satisfying meal is chock-full of nutritious vegetables—even the bread and cake. So if you have a fussy eater who refuses veggies, you can sneak in one or two...and get compliments at the same time! Really.

"Skillet Chicken Supper is a hearty main dish," says Marlene Muckenhirn of Delano, Minnesota. "It's gently spiced with a tasty vegetable medley." Frozen mixed vegetables can be used instead of the peas called for in this recipe.

Cheddar Corn Bread, suggested by Terri Adrian of Lake City, Florida, pleases a crowd with its moist texture and big corn flavor.

The recipe for delicious and penny-pinching Chocolate Potato Cake has been handed down for generations in the family of Charlotte Cleveland from Hobbs, New Mexico. Don't be surprised when members of your family ask for an extra piece.

$1.59 Per Person

Skillet Chicken Supper

1/2 cup all-purpose flour
1/2 teaspoon garlic powder
1/2 teaspoon pepper
  1 broiler/fryer chicken (3 to 4 pounds), cut up
  2 tablespoons vegetable oil
1-3/4 cups water, *divided*
1/2 cup soy sauce
1/2 teaspoon dried oregano
  3 medium red potatoes, cut into 1-inch chunks
  3 large carrots, cut into 1-inch pieces
  3 celery ribs, cut into 1-inch pieces
  1 package (10 ounces) frozen peas

In a resealable plastic bag, combine flour, garlic powder and pepper. Add chicken, one piece at a time, and shake to coat; set the remaining flour mixture aside.

In a large skillet, cook the chicken in oil until browned on all sides; drain. Combine 1-1/4 cups water, soy sauce and oregano; pour over the chicken. Add the vegetables. Bring to a boil; reduce heat. Cover and simmer for 30-40 minutes or until chicken juices run clear. Remove the chicken and vegetables; keep warm.

Combine reserved flour mixture and remaining water until smooth; add to the cooking juices. Bring to a boil; cook and stir for 2 minutes or until thickened. Serve with the chicken and vegetables. **Yield:** 6 servings.

Cheddar Corn Bread

  2 packages (8-1/2 ounces *each*) corn bread/muffin mix
  2 eggs, beaten
1/2 cup milk
1/2 cup plain yogurt
  1 can (14-3/4 ounces) cream-style corn
1/2 cup shredded cheddar cheese

In a bowl, combine the corn bread mix, eggs, milk and yogurt until well blended. Stir in the corn and cheese. Pour into a greased 13-in. x 9-in. x 2-in. baking dish.

Bake at 400° for 18-22 minutes or until a toothpick comes out clean. Cut into squares. Serve warm. **Yield:** 12 servings.

Chocolate Potato Cake

1 cup butter-flavored shortening
2 cups sugar
2 eggs, *separated*
1 cup mashed potatoes
1 teaspoon vanilla extract
2-1/2 cups all-purpose flour
1/2 cup baking cocoa
2-1/2 teaspoons baking powder
1/2 teaspoon *each* ground allspice,
    cinnamon, cloves and nutmeg
3/4 teaspoon salt
1 cup milk
MOCHA FROSTING:
1/3 cup butter, softened

2-2/3 cups confectioners' sugar
2 tablespoons baking cocoa
1/4 teaspoon salt
3 tablespoons strong brewed coffee

In a mixing bowl, cream shortening and sugar. Add egg yolks, one at a time, beating well after each. Add potatoes and vanilla; mix well. Combine dry ingredients; add to creamed mixture alternately with milk. In a small mixing bowl, beat egg whites until soft peaks form; fold into batter.

Pour into a greased and floured 10-in. fluted tube pan. Bake at 325° for 1 to 1-1/4 hours or until a toothpick inserted near center comes out clean. Cool 10 minutes; remove from pan to a wire rack. In a small bowl, combine frosting ingredients until smooth. Frost cooled cake. **Yield:** 16 servings.

The price won't be the first thing that pops into your head when you see the home-style menu we've put together here.

No, you'll be thinking about how good it sounds or how it would satisfy your family on a crisp autumn day. When you do get around to tallying up the cost, you'll feel a smile spread across your face. It's only $1.38 per setting for this trio of dishes shared by three country cooks.

Flavorful Meat Loaf is a firm, hearty loaf with a distinctive taste, thanks to soy sauce and ginger. "This is one recipe I rely on for a satisfying, inexpensive meal," says Sharon Hancock of Belleville, Ontario.

Noodles Florentine is a favorite recommended by Marcia Orlando of Boyertown, Pennsylvania. "With this recipe, you get noodles and a nutritious vegetable in one tasty casserole," Marcia notes.

For a cool and economical treat, try Lemon Graham Freeze from Barbara Husband of Dorchester, Wisconsin. "This light, pleasantly tart dessert is convenient since you make it ahead of time and freeze it," says Barbara.

Flavorful Meat Loaf

✓ Uses less fat, sugar or salt. Includes Nutritional Analysis and Diabetic Exchanges.

1 medium carrot, shredded
1/4 cup chopped onion
2 tablespoons soy sauce
1 teaspoon tomato paste
2 garlic cloves, minced
1/4 teaspoon ground ginger
1/8 teaspoon crushed red pepper flakes
Pepper to taste
1/2 pound ground beef
1/2 pound ground pork

In a bowl, combine the first eight ingredients. Crumble beef and pork over mixture and mix well. Shape into a loaf in an ungreased shallow baking pan.

Bake at 350° for 45-50 minutes or until meat is no longer pink and a meat thermometer reads 160°; drain. Let stand for 10 minutes before slicing. **Yield:** 4 servings.

Nutritional Analysis: One serving (prepared with reduced-sodium soy sauce and 1 pound of lean ground beef instead of beef and pork) equals 215 calories, 353 mg sodium, 41 mg cholesterol, 5 g carbohydrate, 24 g protein, 10 g fat, 1 g fiber. **Diabetic Exchanges:** 3 lean meat, 1 vegetable.

Noodles Florentine

5 cups uncooked medium egg noodles
2 tablespoons butter

2 tablespoons all-purpose flour
1 cup milk
1 package (10 ounces) frozen chopped spinach, thawed and well drained
1/4 teaspoon ground nutmeg
Salt and pepper to taste
1 cup (4 ounces) shredded Swiss cheese

In a large saucepan, cook noodles in water until tender. In another saucepan, melt butter; stir in flour until smooth. Gradually add milk. Bring to a boil; cook and stir for 2 minutes or until thickened. Stir in the spinach, nutmeg, salt and pepper.

Drain noodles. Add to spinach mixture; toss gently to coat. Transfer to a greased shallow 2-qt. baking dish; sprinkle with cheese. Cover and bake at 350° for 20 minutes or until heated through. **Yield:** 4 servings.

Lemon Graham Freeze

1 can (5 ounces) evaporated milk
1/2 cup sugar
2 tablespoons lemon juice
4 drops yellow food coloring, optional
6 whole graham crackers

Place the milk in a mixing bowl; add beaters to bowl. Freeze for 25-30 minutes or until soft crystals form around edges of the bowl. Beat the milk until stiff peaks form. Gradually add the sugar, lemon juice and food coloring if desired; mix well.

Place five graham crackers in an ungreased 11-in. x 7-in. x 2-in. dish; pour the milk mixture over crackers. Crush the remaining graham cracker and sprinkle over top. Cover and freeze until firm. **Yield:** 6 servings.

Making Meat Loaves

Stretch meat loaf—and make it healthier—by adding oatmeal, cooked rice or other quick-cooking or precooked grains or vegetables.

When shaping meat loaves, handle the mixture as little as possible to keep the final product light in texture. Combine all of the ingredients except for the ground meat. Then crumble the meat over the mixture and mix well.

After baking a meat loaf, drain any fat from the pan and let stand for 5 to 10 minutes before slicing.

It's easy to prepare an affordable turkey dinner that your family will gobble up in no time. This inexpensive yet flavor-packed meal is from three terrific cooks. Our Test Kitchen staff estimates the total cost at just 96¢ per setting.

Turkey Tetrazzini is a tasty main dish and a great way to use leftover chicken or turkey, according to Sue Ross of Casa Grande, Arizona. "Everyone loves the spaghetti noodles mixed in," she says.

Lettuce with French Dressing is always a hit at the Mendota, Illinois home of Kim Marie Van Rheenen. "I got this recipe from my mother-in-law when my husband and I first started dating," Kim remembers. "Many years later, it's still our favorite salad."

Just to show that an inexpensive meal can still include dessert, Betty Speth of Vincennes, Indiana shares her recipe for Chewy Almond Cookies. "These old-fashioned cookies are often requested by my children and grandchildren," Betty states. "I'm always happy to oblige."

The unbaked cookie dough can be frozen (well wrapped) for up to 1 year. When ready to bake, remove from the freezer, let stand at room temperature for 15-30 minutes, slice and bake.

96¢ Per Person

Turkey Tetrazzini

- 2 cups broken uncooked spaghetti (2-inch pieces)
- 1 chicken bouillon cube
- 3/4 cup boiling water
- 1 can (10-3/4 ounces) condensed cream of mushroom soup, undiluted
- 1/8 teaspoon celery salt
- 1/8 teaspoon pepper
- 1-1/2 cups cubed cooked turkey
- 1 small onion, finely chopped
- 2 tablespoons diced pimientos, drained
- 1-1/2 cups (6 ounces) shredded cheddar cheese, *divided*
- Red pepper rings, optional

Cook spaghetti according to package directions. Meanwhile, in a bowl, dissolve bouillon in water. Add soup, celery salt and pepper. Drain spaghetti; add to soup mixture. Stir in turkey, onion, pimientos and 1/2 cup of cheese.

Transfer to a greased 8-in. square baking dish. Top with remaining cheese. Bake, uncovered, at 350° for 35-40 minutes or until heated through. Garnish with red pepper rings if desired. **Yield:** 6 servings.

Lettuce with French Dressing

- 1/4 cup plus 2 tablespoons vegetable oil
- 1/4 cup sugar
- 2 tablespoons vinegar
- 2 tablespoons ketchup
- 1/8 teaspoon salt
- Dash garlic powder
- 6 cups torn lettuce

Combine the vegetable oil, sugar, vinegar, ketchup, salt and garlic powder in a jar with a tight-fitting lid; shake well. Serve over lettuce. Refrigerate any leftover dressing. **Yield:** 6 servings (3/4 cup dressing).

Chewy Almond Cookies

- 3 tablespoons butter, softened
- 1 cup packed brown sugar
- 1 egg

1/4 teaspoon vanilla extract
1/4 teaspoon almond extract
1-1/2 cups all-purpose flour
1/4 teaspoon baking soda
1/4 teaspoon ground cinnamon
1/2 cup sliced almonds

In a mixing bowl, cream butter and brown sugar. Add egg and extracts; mix well. Combine flour, baking soda and cinnamon; gradually add to the creamed mixture and mix well. Shape into two 1-in. rolls; wrap each in plastic wrap and refrigerate overnight.

Unwrap; cut into 1/4-in. slices. Place 2 in. apart on greased baking sheets. Sprinkle with almonds. Bake at 350° for 7-10 minutes or until lightly browned. Cool for 2-3 minutes before removing to wire racks. **Yield:** 4-1/2 dozen.

Keen on Greens

Salad greens will last longer if they're washed as soon as you get them home. The easiest way to clean greens is to cut off the bottom to separate the leaves, then put them in a sink or large container full of cold water. Swish the greens around with your hands, then let them stand for a few minutes for any dirt to sink to the bottom.

Dry salad greens by shaking off excess moisture, lay them out on a double layer of paper towels or a clean dish towel, then blot the surface dry.

Serving your family a "centsible" and savory supper is easy as pie!

Three great cooks shared the recipes for this frugal and filling meal, and our Test Kitchen staff estimates a total cost of just $1.01 per setting.

Upside-Down Meat Pie comes from Jennifer Eilts of Central City, Nebraska. "Thanks to the yummy sloppy joe flavor, kids dig in...and adults do, too," Jennifer says. "The recipe's been in my family for years."

Reports Vicky Linn of Corsicana, Texas, "Macaroni Medley Salad is so delicious, folks never believe it starts with a packaged macaroni and cheese box mix."

For a tasty low-cost treat, try sundaes made with Homemade Chocolate Syrup. The recipe comes from Greenfield, Iowa cook Sharon Mensing, who remarks, "I use this microwave recipe so often I have it memorized."

$1.01 Per Serving

Upside-Down Meat Pie

    1 pound ground beef
  1/2 cup chopped celery
  1/2 cup chopped onion
  1/4 cup chopped green pepper
    1 can (10-3/4 ounces) condensed tomato
      soup, undiluted
    1 teaspoon prepared mustard
1-1/2 cups biscuit/baking mix
  1/3 cup water
    3 slices process American cheese,
      halved diagonally
Green pepper rings, optional

In a skillet over medium heat, cook beef, celery, onion and green pepper until the meat is no longer pink and vegetables are tender; drain. Stir in soup and mustard; mix well. Transfer to a greased 9-in. pie plate.

In a bowl, combine the baking mix and water until a soft dough forms. Turn dough onto a lightly floured surface and roll into a 9-in. circle. Place over meat mixture and bake at 425° for 20 minutes or until golden brown.

Cool for 5 minutes. Run a knife around the edge to loosen the biscuit; invert onto a serving platter. Arrange cheese slices in a pinwheel pattern on the top. Garnish with green pepper rings if desired. **Yield:** 6 servings.

Macaroni Medley Salad

    1 package (7-1/4 ounces) macaroni and
      cheese
  1/4 cup milk
  1/4 cup butter
  1/2 cup mayonnaise
    2 tablespoons Dijon mustard
    4 hard-cooked eggs, chopped
    2 medium tomatoes, chopped
    1 small cucumber, peeled and chopped
    2 tablespoons chopped onion
    1 dill pickle, chopped
  1/2 teaspoon salt
  1/8 teaspoon pepper

Prepare macaroni and cheese with milk and butter according to package directions. Place in a large bowl; cool for 15 minutes.

Stir in the mayonnaise and mustard. Fold in the hard-cooked eggs, tomatoes, cucumber, onion, pickle, salt and pepper. Refrigerate until serving. **Yield:** 6 servings.

Homemade Chocolate Syrup

1/2 cup sugar
1 tablespoon baking cocoa
2-1/2 teaspoons cornstarch
1/2 cup water
2 teaspoons butter
1/2 teaspoon vanilla extract
1 quart vanilla ice cream

In a 1-qt. microwave-safe dish, combine sugar, cocoa, cornstarch and water until smooth. Cover; microwave on high 4 minutes or until mixture boils, stirring twice. Stir in butter and vanilla until blended. Serve over ice cream. **Yield:** 6 servings.

Editor's Note: This recipe was tested in an 850-watt microwave.

Incredible Ice Cream

Make your own premium stir-in style of ice cream by adding 1/2 to 3/4 cup of any of the following to a softened pint of your favorite ice cream: crushed cream-filled chocolate cookies; raisins or chopped dried fruit; chopped nuts; chopped fresh fruit; chocolate chunks; miniature marshmallows; chopped chocolate-covered mints. Return ice cream to the freezer for at least 2 hours to refirm.

Use melted ice cream as a tasty topping for puddings, cakes, pies or hot breakfast cereal.

Welcome a group of family and friends into your home for some country cooking that won't make you run to the bank.

The comforting and cost-conscious meal here is from three terrific cooks and costs just $1.46 per setting.

"Stuffed Cube Steaks turn an inexpensive cut of meat into a satisfying main dish," says great-grand-mother Marie Reynolds of Gardner, Massachusetts.

Sweet Peas and Mushrooms, recommended by Wendy Masters of Grand Valley, Ontario, is a special yet simple vegetable dish. "The flavors of the two vegetables really complement each other," says Wendy.

Fresh Peach Cobbler uses late summer's delicious peaches. "I enjoy the taste of nutmeg in this classic dessert," shares Pat Kinghorn of Morrill, Nebraska.

$1.46 Per Person

Stuffed Cube Steaks

    8 cube steaks (about 2 pounds)
1-1/4 teaspoons salt, *divided*
  1/4 teaspoon pepper
  1/2 cup French salad dressing
    1 cup shredded carrot
  3/4 cup finely chopped onion
  3/4 cup finely chopped celery
  1/2 cup finely chopped green pepper
  1/4 cup beef broth
    2 tablespoons vegetable oil
    1 tablespoon cornstarch
  1/4 teaspoon browning sauce, optional

Pound steaks to 1/4-in. thickness. Sprinkle with 1 teaspoon salt and pepper. Place in a greased 13-in. x 9-in. x 2-in. baking dish. Spoon salad dressing over steaks. Cover and chill for 1 hour.

In a saucepan, combine the carrot, onion, celery, green pepper, broth and remaining salt. Cover and cook over medium heat for 6-8 minutes or until tender. Drain, reserving liquid. Spoon 1/4 cup vegetable mixture onto each steak; roll up and secure with toothpicks.

In a large nonstick skillet, brown meat rolls in oil. Cover and simmer for 35-40 minutes or until meat is tender. Remove with a slotted spoon; keep warm.

Combine the cornstarch and reserved cooking liquid until smooth; stir into pan drippings. Bring to a boil; cook and stir for 2 minutes. Add browning sauce if desired. Remove toothpicks from meat rolls; pour sauce over and serve immediately. **Yield:** 8 servings.

Sweet Peas and Mushrooms

    2 packages (10 ounces *each*) frozen peas
    2 cups sliced fresh mushrooms
  1/2 cup chopped onion
  1/4 cup butter
    2 teaspoons sugar
    1 teaspoon salt
Dash pepper

Cook peas according to package directions; drain. Meanwhile, in a skillet, saute mushrooms and onion in butter until onion is crisp-tender. Stir in sugar, salt, pepper and peas. Cover and cook until heated through. **Yield:** 8 servings.

Fresh Peach Cobbler

    2 large peaches, peeled and sliced
1-1/2 cups sugar, *divided*

1/2 cup butter, melted
1 cup all-purpose flour
2 teaspoons baking powder
1/4 teaspoon salt
Dash ground nutmeg
3/4 cup milk

In a large bowl, combine the peaches and 3/4 cup sugar; set aside. Pour the butter into an 8-in. square baking dish.

In another large bowl, combine the flour, baking powder, salt, nutmeg and remaining sugar. Make a well in the center. Pour milk into the well and stir just until combined. Pour over the butter. Top with the peaches. Bake at 375° for 45-50 minutes. **Yield:** 8 servings.

What a Peach

Peaches are native to China. They were brought to the United States in the 1600s and planted along the eastern seaboard. Peaches have been grown commercially in the states since the 1800s.

When buying fresh peaches, choose intensely fragrant fruit that gives slightly to palm pressure. Avoid those that are hard, have soft spots or show signs of greening.

Store ripe peaches in the refrigerator in a plastic bag for up to 5 days.

Want to add spark to your supper without burning cash? Three cooks shared these tasty recipes at a total cost of just 75¢ per setting.

Chili Spaghetti is recommended by Pam Thompson of Girard, Illinois. "My husband often requested that his grandma make this dish," shares Pam.

The recipe for Jalapeno Corn Bread comes from Anita LaRose. "We enjoy the combination of flavors in this golden corn bread," says this Benavides, Texas cook. "It's not dry or crumbly."

Chocolate Bundt Cake is a dessert from Lori Bennett's grandmother. "When I make this yummy, economical cake for my son and husband, it brings back many fond memories for me," says the Greencastle, Indiana cook.

75¢ Per Serving

Chili Spaghetti

- 1 pound ground beef
- 1/2 cup chopped onion
- 2 garlic cloves, minced
- 3 cups tomato juice
- 1 can (16 ounces) kidney beans, rinsed and drained
- 6 ounces spaghetti, broken into 3-inch pieces
- 1 tablespoon Worcestershire sauce
- 2 to 3 teaspoons chili powder
- 1 teaspoon salt
- 1/2 teaspoon pepper

In a skillet over medium heat, cook beef, onion and garlic until meat is no longer pink; drain. Transfer to a greased 2-1/2-qt. baking dish; stir in the remaining ingredients. Cover and bake at 350° for 65-70 minutes or until spaghetti is just tender. Let stand, covered, for 10 minutes. **Yield:** 6 servings.

Jalapeno Corn Bread

- 1 cup cornmeal
- 1/2 cup shredded cheddar cheese
- 2 teaspoons baking powder
- 3/4 teaspoon salt
- 2 eggs, beaten
- 1 can (8-3/4 ounces) cream-style corn
- 1 cup buttermilk
- 1/4 cup vegetable oil
- 1 to 2 tablespoons minced fresh jalapeno peppers

In a bowl, combine cornmeal, cheese, baking powder and salt. Combine the remaining ingredients; stir into cornmeal mixture just until moistened.

Transfer to a greased 9-in. square baking pan. Bake at 350° for 1 hour or until a toothpick inserted near center comes out clean. **Yield:** 9 servings.

Editor's Note: When cutting or seeding hot peppers, use rubber or plastic gloves to protect your hands. Avoid touching your face.

Chocolate Bundt Cake

- 1 cup salad dressing
- 1 cup water
- 2 teaspoons vanilla extract
- 2 cups all-purpose flour
- 1 cup sugar
- 2 tablespoons baking cocoa
- 2 teaspoons baking soda
- 1/4 teaspoon salt
- Confectioners' sugar, optional

In a mixing bowl, combine the salad dressing, water and vanilla. Combine the flour, sugar, cocoa, baking soda and salt. Add to the salad dressing mixture and beat until mixed. Transfer to a greased and floured 10-in. fluted tube pan (the pan will not be full).

Bake at 350° for 35-40 minutes or until a toothpick inserted near the center comes out clean. Cool for 10 minutes; remove from pan to a wire rack. Dust with confectioners' sugar if desired. **Yield:** 12 servings.

Editor's Note: This recipe was tested using Miracle Whip brand salad dressing. Reduced-fat or fat-free Miracle Whip may not be substituted for regular Miracle Whip.

Greasing Pans

The recipe term "grease and flour" refers to sprinkling a greased pan with a small amount of flour, then tapping and rotating the pan or dish until the entire surface is coated with flour. Invert the container over the sink or a waste basket and shake it gently to remove excess flour.

When a chocolate cake recipe calls for greasing and flouring the pan, grease it, then dust with unsweetened cocoa powder.

If holiday spending has stretched your family budget, you'll appreciate this penny-pinching meal. It comes from three great cooks and costs just $1.12 per setting.

Salisbury Steak with Onion Gravy gets high praise from Kim Kidd of New Freedom, Pennsylvania. "This hearty main dish is a favorite at our house," reports Kim. "Servings really warm up my family."

Corn 'n' Broccoli Bake is a sweet, comforting side dish from Betty Sitzman of Wray, Colorado. It's a very creamy casserole that resembles corn pudding. The casserole is a delicious way to get your family to eat their vegetables!

Scrumptious Coconut Pie is an old-fashioned dessert. "I sometimes top warm slices with a sprinkling of cinnamon or nutmeg," notes Virginia Krites from Cridersville, Ohio. "Best of all, the simple pie is so easy to assemble when dinnertime is fast approaching."

$1.12 Per Person

Salisbury Steak with Onion Gravy

  1 egg
  1 can (10-1/2 ounces) condensed French
    onion soup, undiluted, *divided*
  1/2 cup dry bread crumbs
  1/4 teaspoon salt
Pinch pepper
1-1/2 pounds ground beef
  1 tablespoon all-purpose flour
  1/4 cup water
  1/4 cup ketchup
  1 teaspoon Worcestershire sauce
  1/2 teaspoon prepared mustard
  6 cups hot cooked egg noodles
Chopped fresh parsley, optional

In a large bowl, beat the egg. Stir in 1/3 cup of soup, dry bread crumbs, salt and pepper. Crumble beef over mixture and mix gently. Shape into six oval patties. Brown in a skillet over medium heat for 3-4 minutes on each side. Remove and set aside; discard drippings.

In the same skillet, combine flour and water until smooth; add ketchup, Worcestershire sauce, mustard and remaining soup; bring to a boil. Cook and stir for 2 minutes.

Return patties to skillet. Cover and simmer for 15 minutes or until meat is no longer pink. Serve patties and gravy over noodles. Garnish with parsley if desired. **Yield:** 6 servings.

Corn 'n' Broccoli Bake

  1 can (16 ounces) cream-style corn
  1 package (10 ounces) frozen chopped
    broccoli, thawed

  1/2 cup crushed saltines, *divided*
  1 egg, beaten
  1 tablespoon dried minced onion
Dash pepper
  2 tablespoons butter, melted

In a bowl, combine the corn, broccoli, 1/4 cup of saltines, egg, onion and pepper. Place in a greased 1-1/2-qt. baking dish. Combine the butter and remaining saltines; sprinkle over top. Cover and bake at 350° for 45 minutes. **Yield:** 6 servings.

Coconut Pie

  2 cups milk
  1 cup sugar

4 eggs
1/2 cup all-purpose flour
6 tablespoons butter
1 teaspoon vanilla extract
1/2 teaspoon salt
1 cup flaked coconut

In a blender or food processor, combine the milk, sugar, eggs, flour, butter, vanilla extract and salt. Cover and blend for 10 seconds; scrape sides. Blend another 10 seconds. Add the coconut and blend for 2 more seconds.

Pour into a greased 10-in. pie plate. Bake at 350° for 50-55 minutes or until a knife inserted near center comes out clean. Serve warm. Refrigerate leftovers. **Yield:** 6 servings.

Pie Pointers

Refrigerate pies containing dairy products or eggs. Pies made with eggs, milk, sour cream, whipped cream, whipped topping, yogurt or cream cheese should be refrigerated as soon as possible after they've been prepared or about 1 hour after baking.

To cut cream pies more cleanly, dip the knife into a container of hot tap water, then wipe with a damp towel. Repeat after every cut.

Add that just-baked touch by reheating fruit pies in a 300° oven for 10 to 15 minutes.

Even at today's high prices, it is possible to feed your hungry family well for just pennies a person. That's right—pennies a person!

Here, we show you how easy it is to assemble a low-budget menu that's full of down-home flavor to serve family and guests for just 81¢ per serving (including two rolls per person).

Chicken Veggie Casserole is a hot, satisfying complete meal in one dish. The recipe is shared by Martha Balser of Cincinnati, Ohio. "Simply stir together the ingredients and bake," explains Martha.

Wheat Yeast Rolls are light and have a delicate flavor. "They're inexpensive to make from scratch but they taste delicious," says Peggy Starkweather of Gardiner, Montana.

The simply scrumptious recipe for Moist Chocolate Cake comes from Gansevoort, New York cook Janice Arnold.

"This cake is extra chocolaty," Janice assures. The recipe makes the perfect number of servings, so leftovers are never a problem.

81¢ Per Serving

Chicken Veggie Casserole

1 can (10-3/4 ounces) condensed cream of chicken soup, undiluted
1/2 cup milk
1/4 teaspoon dried thyme
1/4 teaspoon salt
1/4 teaspoon pepper
2 cups diced cooked chicken
1 can (16 ounces) whole kernel corn, drained
2 cups frozen cut green beans, thawed
2 cups sliced cooked potatoes

In a large bowl, combine the soup, milk, thyme, salt and pepper. Stir in the chicken, corn, beans and potatoes. Pour mixture into a greased 1-1/2-qt. baking dish.

Bake, uncovered, at 400° for 15 minutes or until heated through. **Yield:** 6 servings.

Wheat Yeast Rolls

✓ Uses less fat, sugar or salt. Includes Nutritional Analysis and Diabetic Exchanges.

1 package (1/4 ounce) active dry yeast
1 cup warm water (110° to 115°)
1/3 cup vegetable oil
3 tablespoons sugar
1 teaspoon salt
1-1/2 cups whole wheat flour
1-1/2 to 2 cups all-purpose flour

In a mixing bowl, dissolve the yeast in water. Add the oil, sugar, salt and whole wheat flour; beat until smooth. Add enough all-purpose flour to form soft dough.

Turn dough onto a floured surface and knead until smooth and elastic, about 6-8 minutes. Place in a greased bowl, turning once to grease the top. Cover dough and let rise in a warm place until doubled, about 1 hour.

Punch the dough down and divide into 12 pieces. Shape into rolls and place 3 in. apart on greased baking sheets. Cover and let rise until doubled, about 30 minutes. Bake at 375° for 15-20 minutes or until rolls are golden. Cool on wire racks. **Yield:** 1 dozen.

Nutritional Analysis: One roll equals 175 calories, 195 mg sodium, 0 cholesterol, 26 g carbohydrate, 4 g protein, 7 g fat. **Diabetic Exchanges:** 1-1/2 starch, 1-1/2 fat.

Moist Chocolate Cake

    1 cup all-purpose flour
    1 cup sugar
    1 cup hot water
    1/2 cup baking cocoa
    1 teaspoon baking powder
    1 teaspoon baking soda
    1 egg
    1/4 cup butter, melted
Confectioners' sugar

In a mixing bowl, combine the first six ingredients. Add egg and butter; mix well. Pour into a greased 8-in. square baking pan. Bake at 350° for 30-35 minutes or until a toothpick inserted near the center comes out clean. Cool. Dust with confectioners' sugar **Yield:** 9 servings.

Shaping Rolls

You can shape dough for rolls in a variety of ways. Instead of just making a traditional round dinner roll, try one of these techniques.

For crescent rolls, roll a portion of dough into a 12-in. circle. Cut into wedges. Roll up from the wide end.

For knot-shaped rolls, shape dough into 3-in. balls. Roll each ball into a rope. Tie a knot; tuck and pinch ends.

For cloverleaf rolls, shape dough into 1-1/2-in. balls. Place three balls in each greased muffin cup.

Chicken and rice have always been economical mealtime mainstays. And with some additional everyday ingredients, you can serve up a flavorful meal fit for a king...without breaking the bank!

The meal here is from three terrific cooks. Our Test Kitchen home economists estimate the total cost at just $1.31 per setting.

Orange Chicken is a tasty way to dress up chicken drumsticks and thighs. "These golden chicken pieces are nicely seasoned with a tangy citrus marinade," explains Rita Goshaw of South Milwaukee, Wisconsin. You probably already have the ingredients on hand, so you can whip up this special chicken for friends and family anytime.

From Golden, Colorado, Sheree Feero sends the recipe for Baked Rice Pilaf. "I'm always in search of inexpensive yet delicious dishes like this one to serve at potlucks," Sheree says. "This fluffy rice dish tastes as good as it looks."

Chocolate Chip Cake, suggested by Sue Reichenbach of Langhorne, Pennsylvania, delightfully combines the flavors of chocolate and cinnamon. Enjoy this dessert with dinner and use leftovers the next day as a handy snack.

$1.31 Per Person

Orange Chicken

  4 chicken legs with thighs (3-1/2 pounds), skin removed
  1 teaspoon salt
  1/8 to 1/4 teaspoon pepper
  3 tablespoons orange juice concentrate
  1 tablespoon honey
  1 teaspoon prepared mustard

Place chicken in a single layer in a greased 13-in. x 9-in. x 2-in. baking pan; sprinkle with salt and pepper. Bake, uncovered, at 375° for 25 minutes.

Meanwhile, combine remaining ingredients. Brush over chicken; bake 15 minutes longer. Brush again; bake 10 minutes more or until the juices run clear. **Yield:** 4 servings.

Baked Rice Pilaf

✓ Uses less fat, sugar or salt. Includes Nutritional Analysis and Diabetic Exchanges.

1-3/4 cups water
  1 cup shredded carrot
  1 cup chopped celery
  3/4 cup uncooked long grain rice
  3 tablespoons minced fresh parsley
  2 tablespoons finely chopped onion
  2 tablespoons butter, melted
  1 tablespoon chicken bouillon granules

Combine all ingredients in an ungreased 8-in. square baking dish. Cover and bake at 375° for 40-45 minutes or until rice is tender, stirring after 25 minutes. **Yield:** 4 servings.

  Nutritional Analysis: One 1/2-cup serving (prepared with margarine and reduced-sodium bouillon) equals 212 calories, 108 mg sodium, 0 cholesterol, 35 g carbohydrate, 4 g protein, 6 g fat. **Diabetic Exchanges:** 2 starch, 1 fat.

Chocolate Chip Cake

  1/2 cup butter, softened
1-1/2 cups sugar, *divided*
  2 eggs
  1 teaspoon vanilla extract
  2 cups all-purpose flour

1-1/2 teaspoons baking powder
1 teaspoon baking soda
1 cup (8 ounces) sour cream
3/4 cup semisweet chocolate chips
1 teaspoon ground cinnamon

In a mixing bowl, cream butter and 1 cup sugar. Add eggs, one at a time, beating well after each addition. Stir in vanilla. Combine flour, baking powder and baking soda; add to the creamed mixture alternately with sour cream.

Spread half of the batter into a greased 9-in. square baking pan. Sprinkle with chocolate chips. Combine cinnamon and remaining sugar and sprinkle over the chocolate chips. Spread with remaining batter. Bake at 350° for 45-50 minutes or until a toothpick inserted near the center comes out clean. **Yield:** 8 servings.

Chicken Clue

To save money, buy chickens whole, cut them up with poultry shears and freeze in portion-size packages. When you purchase whole birds, remember that the larger birds are older and, therefore, will be tougher. Younger chickens are not only more tender, but they also have less fat.

With all the entertaining you do around the holidays, cutting corners isn't easy...especially when it comes to feeding the family. But this palate-pleasing meal proves you can enjoy the flavors of the season without breaking the bank.

This festive supper comes from three great cooks and has a cost of just 95¢ per setting.

Cranberry Turkey Loaf is a delightful alternative to traditional meat loaf, assures Paula Zsiray, a Logan, Utah cook. "It's very moist, and the cranberry sauce gives it a tasty twist," she adds.

The recipe for Glazed Sprouts and Carrots uses simple seasonings to turn this vegetable duo into a special side dish. "It complements any dinner menu," assures Page Alexander of Baldwin City, Kansas.

Mock Apple Pie, suggested by Shirley Hunter of St. Paul, Minnesota, almost magically imitates a real apple pie. "My mother made this dessert often during the Depression, and our guests were always astounded that soda crackers could be such convincing 'apples'," chuckles Shirley.

Cranberry Turkey Loaf

  1 egg
1/2 cup herb-seasoned stuffing mix,
    crushed
3/4 cup whole-berry cranberry sauce,
    divided
1/4 teaspoon salt
1/8 teaspoon pepper
  1 pound ground turkey

In a bowl, beat the egg; add the stuffing mix, 1/4 cup cranberry sauce, salt and pepper. Crumble turkey over mixture and mix well. Spoon into an ungreased 8-in. x 4-in. x 2-in. loaf pan. Bake, uncovered, at 350° for 55-65 minutes or until a meat thermometer reads 165°.

Heat remaining cranberry sauce in a microwave on high for 1 minute or until heated through. Slice turkey loaf; top with cranberry sauce. **Yield:** 4 servings.

Glazed Sprouts and Carrots

✓ Uses less fat, sugar or salt. Includes Nutritional Analysis and Diabetic Exchanges.

1/2 cup water
  1 cup halved fresh brussels sprouts
  2 medium carrots, sliced
1/3 cup orange juice
  1 teaspoon cornstarch
1/2 teaspoon sugar
1/4 teaspoon salt, optional
1/8 teaspoon ground nutmeg

95¢ Per Serving

In a saucepan over medium heat, bring water to a boil. Add vegetables. Cover and simmer for 6-8 minutes or until almost tender; drain and return to pan. In a small bowl, combine orange juice, cornstarch, sugar, salt if desired and nutmeg; stir until smooth. Pour over vegetables. Bring to a boil over medium heat; cook and stir for 2 minutes. **Yield:** 4 servings.

Nutritional Analysis: One 1/2-cup serving (prepared without salt) equals 39 calories, 18 mg sodium, 0 cholesterol, 9 g carbohydrate, 1 g protein, 0 fat. **Diabetic Exchange:** 2 vegetable.

Mock Apple Pie

Pastry for double-crust pie
  18 saltines, halved

1-1/2 cups sugar
1-1/4 cups water
   2 tablespoons lemon juice
   1 teaspoon cream of tartar
1/2 to 1 teaspoon ground cinnamon
1/2 to 1 teaspoon ground nutmcg

Place the bottom of the pastry in a 9-in. pie plate. Layer saltine cracker halves in the pastry shell and set aside.

In a small saucepan, combine all of the remaining ingredients; bring to a boil. Carefully pour over the crackers (filling will be very thin). Cool for 10 minutes.

Cut lattice strips from the remaining pastry; place over the filling. Seal and flute edges. Bake at 400° for 25-30 minutes or until golden brown. **Yield:** 8 servings.

About Brussels Sprouts

Buy small bright-green brussels sprouts with compact heads. Loose-leaved, dull sprouts are over the hill.

Try to buy sprouts the same size so they'll all cook in the same amount of time.

Before cooking, wash and blot them dry. Cut an X in the core of each sprout or slice in half before cooking. Brussels sprouts should be cooked only until crisp-tender. Their color should be a bright, intense green. Overcooking will turn sprouts olive-drab.

To check them for doneness, pierce the stem end with a fork. It should penetrate easily.

If the holidays stretch your family budget, here's a penny-pinching meal you will love. This frugal yet flavorful feast is from three cooks and costs just 99¢ per setting (including two rolls).

Hearty Bean Soup is convenient to simmer all day in a slow cooker, says Alice Schnoor of Arion, Iowa. "Bowl-fulls really warm you up on a cold winter day," attests Alice.

Cornmeal Rolls, from Carol Forcum of Marion, Illinois, are golden and have a subtle cornmeal flavor.

Hot Water Gingerbread is a moist, old-fashioned dessert from country cook Marjorie Green of South Haven, Michigan.

Hearty Bean Soup

3 cups chopped parsnips
2 cups chopped carrots
1 cup chopped onion
1-1/2 cups dry great northern beans
5 cups water
1-1/2 pounds smoked ham hocks *or* ham shanks
2 garlic cloves, minced
2 teaspoons salt
1/2 teaspoon pepper
1/8 to 1/4 teaspoon hot pepper sauce

In a 5-qt. slow cooker, place parsnips, carrots and onion. Top with beans. Add water, ham, garlic, salt, pepper and hot pepper sauce. Cover and cook on high for 6-7 hours or until beans are tender.

Remove meat and bones when cool enough to handle. Cut meat into bite-size pieces and return to slow cooker; heat through. **Yield:** 6 servings.

Cornmeal Rolls

2-1/4 cups warm water (110° to 115°), *divided*
1/3 cup cornmeal
1/4 cup sugar
3 tablespoons vegetable oil
2 teaspoons salt
2 packages (1/4 ounce *each*) active dry yeast
2 eggs
5 to 5-1/2 cups all-purpose flour
Melted butter
Additional cornmeal

In a saucepan, combine 1-3/4 cups water, cornmeal, sugar, oil and salt. Cook and stir over medium heat until mixture boils, about 10 minutes. Cool at room temperature to 120°-130°. Place in a mixing bowl. Dissolve yeast in remaining water; add to cornmeal mixture. Add eggs and mix well. Add enough flour to form a soft dough.

Turn onto a floured surface; knead until smooth

and elastic, about 6-8 minutes. Place in a greased bowl, turning once to grease top. Cover and let rise in a warm place until doubled, about 45-60 minutes.

Punch dough down. Shape into 24 balls. Place on greased baking sheets; brush with butter and sprinkle with cornmeal. Let rise, uncovered, until doubled, about 30 minutes. Bake at 375° for 18-20 minutes or until golden brown. Immediately remove from baking sheet; serve warm. **Yield:** 2 dozen.

Hot Water Gingerbread

1 cup all-purpose flour
1/2 cup sugar
1 teaspoon salt

1 teaspoon ground ginger
1/2 teaspoon baking soda
  1 egg
1/2 cup molasses
1/2 cup hot water
  1 tablespoon butter, softened
TOPPING:
  2 tablespoons sugar
  2 teaspoons ground cinnamon
Whipped topping

Combine flour, sugar, salt, ginger and baking soda; set aside. In a mixing bowl, beat egg, molasses, water and butter until smooth. Gradually add dry ingredients; beat for 1 minute. Pour into a greased 8-in. square baking pan. Combine the sugar and cinnamon; sprinkle evenly over gingerbread.

Bake at 350° for 25 minutes or until a toothpick inserted near the center comes out clean. Cool completely before cutting. Top each square with whipped topping. **Yield:** 9 servings.

A Kernel on Cornmeal

Cornmeal comes in three textures: fine (often called corn flour), medium (the texture most commonly available commercially) and coarse (also known as polenta).

Masa Harina is a special corn flour used to make tortillas and tamales.

Why not welcome family and friends to a casual supper featuring a country meat-and-potatoes meal?

Three creative cooks show how entertaining can be simple and satisfying as well as economical. Their satisfying meal featured here costs just $1.29 per setting!

Country-Fried Steak is a favorite of Betty Claycomb and her husband, Harold, who live in Alverton, Pennsylvania. "This down-home main dish is simple to make yet tastes so delicious," shares Betty.

Chive Carrots have such rich garden-fresh flavor, you'd never guess how inexpensive this side dish is to prepare. Wills Point, Texas cook Dorothy Pritchett says using fresh garlic gives them that great flavor.

In Spencerport, New York, Theresa Evans recalls her grandmother making Dilly Mashed Potatoes for her over the past 30 years. "I just love dill, especially in these potatoes," says Theresa. "You'll agree they're perfect anytime."

Country-Fried Steak

1/2 **cup all-purpose flour**
1/2 **teaspoon salt**
1/2 **teaspoon pepper**
3/4 **cup buttermilk**
  1 **cup crushed saltines**
  4 **cube steaks (1 pound)**
  3 **tablespoons vegetable oil**
  1 **can (10-3/4 ounces) condensed cream of mushroom soup, undiluted**
  1 **cup milk**

In a plastic bag or bowl, combine flour, salt and pepper. Place buttermilk in a shallow bowl. Place saltine crumbs in a plastic bag or bowl. Coat steaks with flour mixture, then dip into buttermilk and coat with crumbs.

In a large skillet over medium-high heat, cook steaks in hot oil for 2-3 minutes on each side or until golden and cooked to desired doneness. Remove and keep warm.

Add soup and milk to skillet; bring to a boil, stirring to loosen browned bits from pan. Serve gravy with steaks. **Yield:** 4 servings.

Chive Carrots

✓ Uses less fat, sugar or salt. Includes Nutritional Analysis and Diabetic Exchanges.

  1 **pound carrots, cut into 2-inch julienne strips**
  1 **garlic clove, minced**
  1 **tablespoon vegetable oil**
  1 **tablespoon stick margarine**

$1.29 Per Serving

  2 **tablespoons minced fresh chives *or* parsley**

In a large skillet, saute the carrots and garlic in oil and margarine for 3 minutes. Reduce heat; cover and cook for 10 minutes or until carrots are crisp-tender. Sprinkle with chives or parsley. Serve immediately. **Yield:** 4 servings.

Nutritional Analysis: One 1/2-cup serving equals 106 calories, 64 mg sodium, 0 cholesterol, 12 g carbohydrate, 1 g protein, 6 g fat. **Diabetic Exchanges:** 2 vegetable, 1 fat.

Dilly Mashed Potatoes

  2 pounds potatoes, peeled and cubed
  2 tablespoons butter, softened
1/4 cup milk
1/4 cup sour cream
1/2 to 3/4 teaspoon dill weed
1/2 to 3/4 teaspoon salt
1/4 teaspoon pepper

Cook potatoes in boiling water until tender; drain.
Mash with remaining ingredients. **Yield:** 4 servings.

Hot Potato Hints

Russets make the best mashed potatoes. Cook the potatoes only until
they're fork-tender; drain immediately so they don't absorb excess moisture.
Mashed potatoes are best served right away,
but you can make them 15 to 20 minutes
ahead and reheat in the microwave.

Two terrific cooks show that it is possible to serve your family a well-balanced meal without spending too much money. Our Test Kitchen staff estimates that the delicious chicken dinner featured here costs just $1.33 per setting!

Chicken Confetti is hearty and delicious with a fresh-tasting sauce. "Before our children grew up and started out on their own, this was a real favorite around our house," remembers Sundra Lewis of Bogalusa, Louisiana.

"Now when the kids come home and bring friends, this main dish is the most requested," adds Sundra. "No one can resist the tender chicken simmering in a savory homemade tomato sauce. This dish is a definite budget-stretcher."

Sundra also shares her recipe for Dilled Zucchini. "These super squash couldn't be easier to prepare, and their mild flavor goes so well with the chicken," she shares. "I often rely on this side dish when I have a bumper crop of home-grown zucchini to use up."

From Winnsboro, Texas, Dorothy Collins sends the recipe for Orange Whip. "It's a wonderfully light and refreshing dessert," she assures, "especially during the warm summer months."

$1.33 Per Person

Chicken Confetti

     1 broiler-fryer chicken (3 pounds),
       cut up
     1 teaspoon salt, *divided*
   1/4 teaspoon pepper
     2 tablespoons vegetable oil
     1 medium onion, chopped
     1 garlic clove, minced
     2 cans (14-1/2 ounces *each*) diced
       tomatoes, undrained
     1 can (8 ounces) tomato sauce
     1 can (6 ounces) tomato paste
 1-1/2 teaspoons dried basil
     1 package (7 ounces) spaghetti, cooked
       and drained

Sprinkle chicken with 1/2 teaspoon salt and pepper. In a large skillet over medium heat, brown chicken in oil. Remove chicken and set aside. Reserve 1 tablespoon drippings in skillet; add onion and garlic. Saute until tender.

Add tomatoes, sauce, paste, basil and remaining salt; bring to a boil. Return chicken to skillet. Reduce heat; cover and simmer for 60-70 minutes or until meat is tender. Serve over spaghetti. **Yield:** 6 servings.

Dilled Zucchini

✓ Uses less fat, sugar or salt. Includes Nutritional Analysis and Diabetic Exchanges.

     3 medium zucchini, halved lengthwise
     1 tablespoon stick margarine,
       melted
   1/4 teaspoon dill weed
Salt and pepper to taste, optional

Place zucchini in a skillet and cover with water; bring to a boil over medium heat. Cook until tender, about 12-14 minutes. Drain; brush with margarine. Sprinkle with dill and salt and pepper if desired. **Yield:** 6 servings.

Nutritional Analysis: One serving (prepared without salt) equals 28 calories, 25 mg sodium, 0 cholesterol, 2 g carbohydrate, 1 g protein, 2 g fat. **Diabetic Exchanges:** 1/2 vegetable, 1/2 fat.

Orange Whip

1 envelope unflavored gelatin
1/3 cup sugar
1/8 teaspoon salt
1-3/4 cups hot orange juice (150°)
3/4 cup whipped topping

In a mixing bowl, combine the gelatin, sugar and salt; add the orange juice and stir until the gelatin dissolves. Chill until slightly thickened, about 1-1/2 hours.

Beat on low speed until light and fluffy. Spoon into dessert dishes; chill until firm. Top each with a dollop of whipped topping before serving. **Yield:** 6 servings.

Chicken Tips

Poultry shears are often much easier to use than a knife when cutting up chicken.

Brown chicken over medium heat; cooking over high heat can cause the outside meat to turn stringy.

Both under- and over-cooking will result in a tough chicken. For the most tender results, cook boneless chicken to an internal temperature of 170° and bone-in chicken to a temperature of 180°.

Eating light—yet still satisfying—meals during warmer months means a break for your pocketbook.

Here, three talented cooks show how easy it is to put together a tempting low-budget menu for just $1.30 a setting (including two muffins per person) that's sure to please the whole family.

Roast Beef and Potato Salad comes from Joanna Lonnecker of Omaha, Nebraska. "This hearty flavor-packed salad is a favorite of the 'meat-and-potatoes' members of our family," shares Joanna. "I like to serve it as a light main course throughout the year."

Cornmeal Cheese Muffins are preferred over a pan of plain corn bread at the Dallas, Oregon home of Sherri Gentry. "These cheesy muffins are moist, tasty and favored by everyone who samples them," she says.

"Banana Custard Pudding is an easy dessert you can quickly whip up any time your family requests it," declares Hazel Fritchie of Palestine, Illinois. "So be sure to keep this recipe and its ingredients on hand."

$1.30 Per Serving

Roast Beef and Potato Salad

 2 cups cubed cooked roast beef
 2 cups cubed peeled potatoes, cooked
 1/2 cup chopped green pepper
 1/2 cup thinly sliced celery
 1/4 cup chopped onion
 2 tablespoons chopped pimientos
 1/3 cup vegetable oil
 2 to 3 tablespoons vinegar
 2 teaspoons prepared horseradish
 1/2 teaspoon salt
 1/8 teaspoon pepper
Lettuce leaves
 2 tablespoons chopped fresh parsley

In a large bowl, combine beef, potatoes, green pepper, celery, onion and pimientos. Combine the next five ingredients; mix well. Pour over beef mixture and toss to coat.

Cover and refrigerate for at least 1 hour. Serve on lettuce; sprinkle with parsley. **Yield:** 4 servings.

Cornmeal Cheese Muffins

1-1/2 cups all-purpose flour
 1/2 cup yellow cornmeal
 1/4 cup sugar
 1 tablespoon baking powder
 3/4 teaspoon salt
 1/2 cup small-curd cottage cheese
 3/4 cup milk
 1/4 cup vegetable oil
 1 egg

 1/2 cup shredded cheddar cheese
 1/2 teaspoon dried thyme

In a mixing bowl, combine flour, cornmeal, sugar, baking powder and salt. In another bowl, mash cottage cheese with a fork; add milk, oil and egg. Add to dry ingredients; stir just until moistened. Fold in cheddar cheese and thyme.

Fill greased or paper-lined muffin cups three-fourths full. Bake at 400° for 20-25 minutes or until golden brown. Cool in pan 5 minutes before removing to a wire rack. **Yield:** 1 dozen.

Banana Custard Pudding

 1/2 cup sugar
 1 tablespoon cornstarch

1/8 teaspoon salt
1-1/2 cups milk
   3 egg yolks, beaten
   1 teaspoon vanilla extract
   1 medium firm banana, sliced
Fresh mint, optional

In a saucepan, combine sugar, cornstarch and salt. Gradually add milk; cook and stir over medium heat until mixture comes to a boil. Cook and stir 2 minutes longer.

Stir a small amount into the egg yolks, then return all to the pan. Cook and stir until thickened. Remove from the heat and stir in vanilla extract. Chill for 1 hour.

Just before serving, fold the banana slices into the pudding. Garnish with fresh mint if desired. **Yield:** 4 servings.

Just Desserts

For a quick dessert, horizontally cut a peeled banana and place it, cut side up, on a baking sheet coated with nonstick cooking spray. Sprinkle the banana halves with brown sugar, cinnamon and nutmeg, and broil until the sugar is bubbly.

Or freeze banana slices on a baking sheet coated with nonstick cooking spray until hard. Dip the slices in melted chocolate after freezing, then let harden before transferring them to a freezer-proof plastic bag and storing in the freezer.

Eating on the cheap is easy when you rely on a family-favorite casserole, refreshing salad and easy-to-make cookies.

The inexpensive yet enticing meal here costs just 89¢ per setting.

Tuna Mushroom Casserole is a rich-tasting main dish. The recipe was sent by Connie Moore of Medway, Ohio, who says, "I usually serve this casserole when I'm short on time and we need something hearty and comforting in a hurry. It really fills the bill."

Snap Salad comes from Rick Leeser of Medford, Oregon. "This colorful, refreshing salad is a snap to make and is enjoyable with any meal," he says. Crisp cucumbers are the star of this zippy marinated medley.

Vanilla Wafer Cookies are an irresistible treat, comments Edith Mac Beath of Gaines, Pennsylvania. They're a wonderful way to round out an inexpensive menu.

89¢ Per Person

Tuna Mushroom Casserole

- 1 package (12 ounces) wide noodles, cooked and drained
- 2 cans (6 ounces *each*) tuna, drained and flaked
- 1 can (4 ounces) mushroom stems and pieces, drained
- 1 can (10-3/4 ounces) condensed cream of mushroom soup, undiluted
- 1-1/3 cups milk
- 1/2 teaspoon salt
- 1/4 teaspoon pepper
- 1/2 cup crushed saltines
- 3 tablespoons butter, melted
Paprika, tomato slices and fresh thyme, optional

In a large bowl, combine noodles, tuna and mushrooms. Combine the soup, milk, salt and pepper; pour over noodle mixture and mix well. Pour into a greased 2-1/2-qt. baking dish. Combine saltines and butter; sprinkle over noodles.

Bake, uncovered, at 350° for 35-45 minutes or until heated through. If desired, sprinkle with paprika and garnish with tomato and thyme. **Yield:** 6 servings.

Snap Salad

- 2 medium cucumbers, halved and thinly sliced
- 2 medium carrots, julienned
- 1/4 cup diced onion
- 2 tablespoons raisins
- 3/4 cup water
- 1/4 cup vinegar
- 2 tablespoons sugar
- 1/2 teaspoon salt
- 1/4 teaspoon pepper
- 1/4 teaspoon paprika

In a large bowl, combine cucumbers, carrots, onion and raisins. Combine the remaining ingredients; pour over the cucumber mixture.

Cover and refrigerate for at least 6 hours. Serve salad with a slotted spoon. **Yield:** 6 servings.

Vanilla Wafer Cookies

- 1/2 cup butter, softened
- 1 cup sugar

1 egg
1 tablespoon vanilla extract
1-1/3 cups all-purpose flour
3/4 teaspoon baking powder
1/4 teaspoon salt

In a mixing bowl, cream the butter and sugar. Beat in the egg and vanilla extract. In another bowl, combine the flour, baking powder and salt; add to creamed mixture and mix well.

Drop dough by teaspoonfuls 2 in. apart onto ungreased baking sheets. Bake at 350° for 12-15 minutes or until the edges of the cookies are golden brown. Remove cookies to a wire rack to cool completely. Store in an airtight container. **Yield:** about 3-1/2 dozen.

Tuna Tidbits

Canned tuna is precooked and can be water- or oil-packed. It comes in three grades, the best being solid or fancy (large pieces), followed by chunk (smaller pieces) and flaked (bits and pieces).

Water-packed tuna not only contains fewer calories than oil-packed, but it also has a fresher flavor.

If you're making tuna sandwiches, don't waste money on solid- or chunk-style tuna, since the mixture will be broken up anyway.

If you're pinching your pennies to save up for future holiday purchases, you don't have to forgo flavorful foods.

Three experienced cooks share their recipes for a filling—yet cost-conscious—meal with an estimated total cost of just 87¢ per setting.

After-Thanksgiving Salad is a delightful and unexpected way to use leftover turkey. "This hearty salad is so delicious and pretty," remarks Betty Peel of Milford, Ohio.

Quick Corn Chowder is recommended by Diane Brewster of Highland, New York. "When my husband and I decided I'd stay home with our new baby, his salary had to be stretched pretty thin," Diane recalls. "I became an expert at preparing meals with more 'sense' than dollars! This chowder is a family favorite."

Popovers make even an inexpensive meal fun and special. The recipe comes from Lourdes Dewick of Fort Lauderdale, Florida. "They're light, airy and delicious," says Lourdes.

87¢ Per Serving

After-Thanksgiving Salad

3-1/2 cups diced cooked turkey
    4 celery ribs, sliced
    4 green onions, sliced
1/2 cup chopped pecans, toasted
1/2 cup chopped sweet red pepper
1/2 cup mayonnaise
    1 tablespoon lemon juice
1/4 teaspoon dill weed *or* dried tarragon
1/4 teaspoon salt
1/8 teaspoon pepper
Lettuce leaves, optional

In a large bowl, combine turkey, celery, onions, pecans and red pepper. Combine mayonnaise, lemon juice, dill, salt and pepper; stir into turkey mixture. Refrigerate until serving. Serve on lettuce if desired. **Yield:** 6 servings.

Quick Corn Chowder

    1 bacon strip, diced
    1 medium onion, diced
    1 can (14-1/2 ounces) chicken broth
    2 cups water
    2 large potatoes, peeled and diced
1/2 teaspoon salt
1/4 teaspoon pepper
    1 can (15 ounces) whole kernel corn, drained
    1 cup milk, *divided*
1/4 cup all-purpose flour
Chopped fresh parsley, optional

In a 3-qt. saucepan, cook bacon until crisp; remove to paper towel to drain. Saute the onion in drippings until tender. Add the broth, water and potatoes; bring to a boil. Reduce heat; cover and simmer for 15 minutes or until the potatoes are tender. Add salt and pepper; mix well. Add the corn and 3/4 cup milk. Combine the flour and remaining milk until smooth; add to soup.

Bring to a boil; cook and stir for 2 minutes. Garnish with bacon and parsley if desired. **Yield:** 6 servings.

Popovers

    1 tablespoon shortening
    2 eggs
    1 cup milk
    1 tablespoon butter, melted

1 cup all-purpose flour
1/2 teaspoon salt

Using 1/2 of teaspoon shortening for each cup, grease the bottom and sides of six 6-oz. custard cups or the cups of a popover pan. Place custard cups on a 15-in. x 10-in. x 1-in. baking pan and set aside.

In a mixing bowl, beat eggs; blend in milk and butter. Beat in flour and salt until smooth (do not overbeat). Fill cups half full.

Bake at 450° for 15 minutes. Reduce heat to 350°; bake 30 minutes longer or until popovers are very firm.

Remove from the oven and prick each popover to allow steam to escape. Serve immediately. **Yield:** 6 servings.

Popover Pointers

Unlike most other breads, popovers are leavened by eggs and steam. They're very easy and inexpensive to mix and bake.

It's important to leave the oven door shut during the first 20 minutes of baking. Drafts can easily collapse popovers.

Bake popovers until they're nicely browned and firm to the touch. Under-baking can cause popovers to deflate after they're removed from the oven. When done, remove from oven and prick in several places with a fork.

The frugal—yet flavorful—meal here goes to show you can make your bunch a terrific lunch without feeling a financial crunch. Three talented cooks sent the recipes for this meal estimated at a total cost of just 64¢ per setting (which includes two cookies per person).

Double-Decker Cheese Melt, shared by Leslie Eisenbraun of Columbiana, Ohio, is a recipe that's easy to make and deliciously different. "Whenever I serve these tasty sandwiches, my family looks for more," remarks Leslie.

Turkey Noodle Soup, from Margaret Shauers of Great Bend, Kansas, is hearty and flavorful. Margaret shares, "I use leftover turkey and the carcass to prepare this soup—a little goes a long way."

An inexpensive meal can still include dessert, assures Dottie LaPierre of Woburn, Massachusetts, who shares the recipe for simple Sugar 'n' Spice Cookies. Says Dottie, "These sweet and tart cookies are a treat."

64¢ Per Person

Double-Decker Cheese Melt

    1 cup (4 ounces) shredded cheddar cheese
1/4 cup butter, softened
    1 egg
1/2 teaspoon garlic salt
1/2 teaspoon onion salt
    6 slices white bread
Paprika, optional

In a food processor, blend cheese and butter. Add egg, garlic salt and onion salt; process for 1 minute or until creamy. Spread 2 tablespoons on each slice of bread.

Stack two slices of bread, cheese side up, for each sandwich; sprinkle with paprika if desired. Cut sandwiches in half diagonally. Place on an ungreased baking sheet. Bake at 400° for 10-15 minutes or until golden and bubbly. **Yield:** 6 servings.

Turkey Noodle Soup

    9 cups homemade turkey *or* chicken broth
    4 medium carrots, shredded
    3 celery ribs, sliced
    1 medium onion, chopped
    1 teaspoon rubbed sage
1/2 teaspoon pepper
    3 whole cloves
    1 bay leaf
    2 cups diced cooked turkey
    1 cup uncooked macaroni
1/4 cup chopped fresh parsley

In a large kettle or Dutch oven, combine the first six ingredients. Tie cloves and bay leaf in a cheesecloth bag and add to kettle; bring to a boil. Reduce heat; cover and simmer for 1 hour. Add the turkey, macaroni and parsley; cover and simmer for 15-20 minutes or until macaroni is tender and soup is heated through. Discard spice bag. **Yield:** 6 servings (3 quarts).

Sugar 'n' Spice Cookies

    3/4 cup shortening
    1 cup sugar
    1 egg
1/4 cup molasses
    2 cups all-purpose flour
    1 teaspoon baking soda
1-1/2 teaspoons ground ginger
    1 teaspoon ground cinnamon
    3/4 teaspoon ground cloves

1/2 teaspoon salt
LEMON FROSTING:
  2 cups confectioners' sugar
  3 tablespoons butter, softened
  1 teaspoon grated lemon peel
  3 to 4 tablespoons lemon juice

In a mixing bowl, cream shortening and sugar. Add egg; mix well. Beat in molasses. Combine dry ingredients; add to creamed mixture and mix well. Drop by rounded teaspoonfuls onto greased baking sheets. Bake at 350° for 8-10 minutes. Remove to wire racks; cool.

For frosting, cream sugar, butter and lemon peel in a mixing bowl. Gradually add lemon juice, beating until frosting reaches desired spreading consistency. Frost the cooled cookies. **Yield:** about 4-1/2 dozen.

Super Soup

If you can, always make homemade soups a day ahead of time and refrigerate them overnight. The extra time allows the flavors to meld and heighten. Refrigerating soups before serving also allows any fat to float to the surface and solidify, making it easy to lift off before the soup's reheated.

Pasta in soup can turn mushy when left in the broth too long. The best kind of pasta to use is made with 100% semolina flour. Small compact shapes stay firm better than noodle-style pasta.

It looks like a million dollars. But this hearty meal is mouth-watering example of the fact that with the right combination of ingredients, you don't have to give up fully enjoying food to eat inexpensively.

Three wonderful cooks show how easy it is to put together a low-budget menu perfect to serve family or guests for just $1.04 per setting.

Lemony Salmon Patties is an impressive main dish from Lorice Britt of Severn, North Carolina. "With the tasty salmon and zippy lemon sauce, my family finds these patties simply delicious," Lorice says.

Zucchini Pancakes are shared by Charlotte Goldberg of Honey Grove, Pennsylvania. "They're very tasty and easy to make," remarks Charlotte. "And they're a nice change of pace from potato pancakes."

For a sweet, old-fashioned dessert, try Apple Brown Betty from Florence Palmer of Marshall, Illinois.

Florence says she can whip up this tasty treat in no time. And she asserts, "It costs little to prepare, but it's big on flavor."

$1.04 Per Serving

Lemony Salmon Patties

1 can (14-3/4 ounces) pink salmon, drained, skin and bones removed
3/4 cup milk
1 cup soft bread crumbs
1 egg, beaten
1 tablespoon chopped fresh parsley
or 1 teaspoon dried parsley flakes
1 teaspoon minced onion
1/2 teaspoon Worcestershire sauce
1/4 teaspoon salt
1/8 teaspoon pepper
LEMON SAUCE:
2 tablespoons butter
4 teaspoons all-purpose flour
3/4 cup milk
2 tablespoons lemon juice
1/4 teaspoon salt
1/8 to 1/4 teaspoon cayenne pepper

In a bowl, combine the first nine ingredients; mix well. Spoon into eight greased muffin cups, using 1/4 cup in each. Bake at 350° for 45 minutes or until browned.

Meanwhile, melt the butter in a saucepan; stir in the flour to form a smooth paste. Gradually stir in the milk; bring to a boil over medium heat, stirring constantly. Cook for 2 minutes or until mixture is thickened.

Remove from the heat; stir in the lemon juice, salt and cayenne pepper. Serve sauce over patties. **Yield:** 4 servings.

Zucchini Pancakes

1-1/2 cups shredded zucchini
1 egg, lightly beaten
2 tablespoons biscuit/baking mix
3 tablespoons grated Parmesan cheese
Dash pepper
1 tablespoon vegetable oil

In a bowl, combine the zucchini, egg, biscuit mix, parmesan cheese and pepper. Heat oil in a skillet over medium heat; drop batter by 1/4 cupfuls and flatten.

Fry until pancakes are golden brown in color, then turn and cook the other side also until golden brown. **Yield:** 4 servings.

Apple Brown Betty

    4 slices white bread, toasted
    3 cups sliced peeled baking apples
  1/2 cup sugar
  1/2 cup packed brown sugar
    1 teaspoon ground cinnamon
  1/4 cup butter, melted
  1/2 cup half-and-half cream

Tear toast into bite-size pieces; place in a greased
1-1/2-qt. baking dish. Top with apples. Combine
sugars and cinnamon; sprinkle over apples. Drizzle
with butter.

  Cover and bake at 350° for 1 hour, stirring after
30 minutes. Serve warm with half-and-half cream.
Yield: 4 servings.

Stuffed Squash

  Zucchini is wonderful stuffed and
baked. Cut it in half lengthwise,
then scoop the flesh out of the center, leaving a 1/2-inch shell. Chop the
zucchini flesh and combine with sauteed
onions, bell peppers and bread crumbs. Add
some chopped seeded tomatoes, season to
taste and fill the zucchini cavities. Sprinkle
with grated cheese and bake at 400° for about
30 minutes.

  You can also stuff zucchini halves with a
meat and rice filling.

If you're trying to stretch the family budget, here's a great way to make a penny-pinching meal everyone will appreciate.

The enjoyably economical feast here is from three great cooks. The total cost is estimated at just $1.15 per setting.

Pork Stroganoff is a creamy, comforting main dish from Janice Mitchell of Aurora, Colorado. "It's a nice change of pace from the more traditional beef Stroganoff," says Janice.

Broccoli in Herbed Butter, shared by Norma Apel of Dubuque, Iowa, dresses up plain broccoli.

Dill Biscuits are quick to prepare and easy on your pocketbook, assures Marcille Meyer of Battle Creek, Nebraska.

Pork Stroganoff

✓ Uses less fat, sugar or salt. Includes Nutritional Analysis and Diabetic Exchanges.

1-1/2 pounds pork stew meat, cut into 1-1/2-inch cubes
1-1/2 cups water, *divided*
1 teaspoon instant chicken bouillon granules
2 teaspoons paprika
1 cup chopped onion
1 garlic clove, minced
1 tablespoon cornstarch
3/4 cup sour cream
2 tablespoons snipped fresh parsley
1 package (12 ounces) noodles, cooked and drained

In a saucepan coated with nonstick cooking spray, brown pork; drain. Remove meat and set aside. In the same pan, bring 1-1/4 cups water, bouillon and paprika to a boil. Add pork, onion and garlic. Reduce heat; cover and simmer 45 minutes or until meat is tender.

Combine cornstarch and remaining water; gradually add to pan, stirring constantly. Bring to a boil; cook and stir 2 minutes or until thickened. Remove from heat; stir in sour cream and parsley. Serve over noodles. **Yield:** 6 servings.

Nutritional Analysis: One serving (prepared with reduced-sodium bouillon and reduced-fat sour cream and without noodles) equals 251 calories, 99 mg sodium, 76 mg cholesterol, 8 g carbohydrate, 30 g protein, 12 g fat. **Diabetic Exchanges:** 4 lean meat, 1/2 starch.

Broccoli in Herbed Butter

✓ Uses less fat, sugar or salt. Includes Nutritional Analysis and Diabetic Exchanges.

1 pound fresh broccoli, cut into spears

2 tablespoons stick margarine
1-1/2 teaspoons lemon juice
1-1/2 teaspoons finely chopped onion
1/4 teaspoon salt, optional
1/8 teaspoon *each* dried thyme, marjoram and savory

Cook broccoli until crisp-tender. Melt butter; add lemon juice, onion, salt if desired and herbs. Drain broccoli and place in a serving dish. Add butter mixture; stir to coat. **Yield:** 6 servings.

Nutritional Analysis: One serving (prepared without salt) equals 51 calories, 42 mg sodium, 0 cholesterol, 3 g carbohydrate, 2 g protein, 4 g fat. **Diabetic Exchanges:** 1 fat, 1/2 vegetable.

Dill Biscuits

1/4 cup butter, melted
1 tablespoon finely chopped onion
1 teaspoon dill weed
1 tube (10 ounces) refrigerated buttermilk
biscuits

In a bowl, combine the butter, onion and dill weed. Cut the biscuits in half lengthwise; toss in the butter mixture.

Arrange the biscuit halves in a single layer in an ungreased 9-in. square baking pan. Bake at 450° for 8-10 minutes or until the biscuits are golden brown in color. Serve warm. **Yield:** 6 servings.

Superb Herbs

Dried herbs have a stronger, more concentrated flavor than fresh herbs, but they quickly lose their pungency.

The biggest enemies of dried herbs are air, light and heat. Store dried herbs in a cool dark place for up to 6 months. After 3 months, it's best to refrigerate them.

If using dried herbs instead of fresh, substitute 1 teaspoon for each tablespoon fresh.

Here's another meal that will make everybody happy—you…your family…and your household budget manager!

Three creative cooks show how easy it is to put together a low-budget menu for just $1.18 per setting (which includes two thick slices of bread per person).

Spaghetti with Homemade Turkey Sausage is a savory and satisfying main dish with rich flavor from Shirley Goodson of West Allis, Wisconsin.

Sesame French Bread bakes into crunchy golden loaves, according to Peggy Van Arsdale from Trenton, New Jersey. "The recipe yields 2 loaves, so you'll have plenty to pass around," says Peggy.

Squash and Pepper Saute, from June Formanek of Belle Plaine, Iowa, is tasty and beautiful, plus it's a great way to use your zucchini harvest.

$1.18 Per Serving

Spaghetti with Homemade Turkey Sausage

1 pound ground turkey
1 teaspoon fennel seed, crushed
1 teaspoon water
1/2 teaspoon salt
1/2 teaspoon pepper
1 jar (27 ounces) spaghetti sauce
12 ounces spaghetti, cooked and drained

In a bowl, combine turkey, fennel seed, water, salt and pepper. Refrigerate overnight. Crumble into bite-size pieces; cook in a skillet over medium heat until meat is no longer pink. Add spaghetti sauce and heat through. Serve over hot cooked spaghetti. **Yield:** 6 servings.

Sesame French Bread

2 packages (1/4 ounce *each*) active dry yeast
2-1/2 cups warm water (110° to 115°)
2 tablespoons sugar
2 tablespoons vegetable oil
2 teaspoons salt
6 to 6-1/2 cups all-purpose flour
Cornmeal
1 egg white
1 tablespoon water
2 tablespoons sesame seeds

In a large mixing bowl, dissolve yeast in warm water. Add sugar, oil, salt and 4 cups of flour; beat until smooth. Add enough remaining flour to form a soft dough.

Turn onto a floured surface; knead until smooth and elastic, about 6-8 minutes. Place in a greased bowl, turning once to grease top. Cover and let rise in a warm place until doubled, about 1 hour.

Punch dough down. Divide in half. Roll each half into a 15-in. x 10-in. rectangle. Roll up from a long side; seal well. Place with seam side down on a greased baking sheet sprinkled with cornmeal. Beat egg white and water; brush over loaves. Sprinkle with sesame seeds. Cover with plastic wrap sprayed with nonstick cooking spray; let rise until nearly doubled, about 30 minutes.

With a very sharp knife, make four shallow diagonal cuts across the tops of the loaves. Bake at 400° for 25 minutes or until lightly browned. Remove bread from pan and cool on a wire rack. **Yield:** 2 loaves.

Squash and Pepper Saute

2 medium yellow squash, sliced
2 medium zucchini, sliced
1 medium sweet red pepper, julienned
1/4 cup olive oil
1 envelope (.7 ounce) Italian salad
  dressing mix
3 tablespoons red wine vinegar

In a large skillet over medium-high, stir-fry the yellow squash, zucchini and sweet red pepper in oil until crisp-tender, about 3-4 minutes. Sprinkle with salad dressing mix and toss to coat. Stir in the red wine vinegar and mix well. **Yield:** 6 servings.

Pass the Pasta!

There's no need to break long pasta into shorter pieces to fit into the pot. Simply set it in boiling water and, as it softens, ease it around and down into the pan.

Be sure to thoroughly drain cooked pasta. Excess cooking water clinging to the pasta will dilute the sauce.

If cooked pasta sticks together, spritz it gently with hot running water, then drain.

Using recipes that call for ground beef is one of the most economical ways to cook. And there's nothing more fun and flavorful than a juicy hamburger. But instead of preparing the same old burger, how about trying this mouth-watering version?

This delicious meal was put together by three great cooks and costs just 98¢ per setting.

Chili Burgers are hearty, zippy sandwiches shared by Dolores Skrout of Summerhill, Pennsylvania. These burgers are definitely a crowd pleaser. "People are pleasantly surprised to find beans in this recipe," Dolores notes.

Garden Potato Salad puts a fresh-tasting spin on traditional potato salad. "This zesty side dish disappears quickly," says Caroline Weese of Greybull, Wyoming, "especially when I take it to summertime picnics, potlucks and other gatherings."

Hot Apple Sundaes make a comforting dessert. The orange flavor complements the light cinnamon-apple taste. These sundaes are a perfect way to round out your penny-pinching menu, assures Betty Matthews of South Haven, Michigan.

98¢ Per Person

Chili Burgers

- 1 pound ground beef
- 1 can (16 ounces) kidney beans, rinsed and drained
- 1 can (10-3/4 ounces) condensed tomato soup, undiluted
- 1 cup chopped celery
- 1/2 cup chopped green pepper
- 1/2 cup chopped onion
- 1/4 cup ketchup
- 1 tablespoon brown sugar
- 1 teaspoon chili powder
- 1/2 teaspoon ground mustard
- 1/2 teaspoon salt
- 1/4 teaspoon pepper
- 1/8 teaspoon cayenne pepper
- 1/8 teaspoon garlic powder
- 12 hamburger buns, split

In a saucepan over medium heat, cook beef until no longer pink; drain. Add beans, soup, celery, green pepper, onion, ketchup, brown sugar and seasonings; bring to a boil. Reduce heat; cover and simmer for 30-40 minutes or until vegetables are tender. Serve on buns. **Yield:** 12 servings.

Garden Potato Salad

- 1-1/2 pounds red potatoes, quartered
- 3/4 pound fresh green beans, halved
- 10 cherry tomatoes, halved
- 1 small onion, chopped
DRESSING:
- 1/2 cup olive oil
- 1/4 cup cider vinegar
- 2 tablespoons lemon juice
- 2 tablespoons Dijon mustard
- 2 teaspoons dried basil
- 2 garlic cloves, minced
- 1-1/4 teaspoons sugar
- 1/4 teaspoon hot pepper sauce

In a saucepan, cook the potatoes in boiling salted water for 8 minutes. Add the green beans and return to a boil. Cook for 5 minutes or until the beans are crisp-tender and the potatoes are just tender; drain and cool.

Place in a large bowl; add the tomatoes and onion. Combine dressing ingredients; pour over the salad and toss to coat. Refrigerate until serving. **Yield:** 12 servings.

Hot Apple Sundaes

    1 cup sugar
    1 cup orange juice
    1/2 cup lemon juice
    1/2 teaspoon ground cinnamon
    10 cups sliced peeled apples
    1-1/2 quarts vanilla ice cream

In a saucepan over medium heat, bring sugar, juices and cinnamon to a boil. Reduce heat; simmer, uncovered, for 5 minutes. Add apples and return to a boil.

Reduce heat; cover and simmer for 15 minutes or until the apples are tender. Serve sauce warm over vanilla ice cream. **Yield:** 12 servings (5 cups topping).

Potato Salad Suggestions

Round red and round white potatoes (also called boiling potatoes) have a waxy flesh with less starch and more moisture than russet potatoes, making them better suited for boiling. They also can be roasted or fried.

If you're using potatoes for a recipe with the skin on, first use a vegetable brush to scrub them well.

Potatoes for potato salad will absorb more dressing if you dress them while they're hot, then refrigerate.

How much does a meal that includes a main dish, soup and bread cost? With this one, a lot less than you probably think. The total cost for the following meal is estimated at just 79¢ per setting—and that includes two slices of bread per person.

Fresh from the garden, Creamy Tomato Soup is from Sue Gronholz of Columbus, Wisconsin. "I can tomato juice, which makes this recipe even more economical," Sue notes. "My husband really enjoys this soup, so I often pack it in his lunch."

From Essex Junction, Vermont, Jackie Gavin sends her favorite recipe for delicious Oatmeal Wheat Bread. "My mother taught me to make this bread when I was 10 years old," she remembers. "And of the many kinds of breads I've baked over the years, this one is my favorite. It tastes marvelous and it's good for you!"

Tuna Pasta Salad is a tasty salad shared by Pat Kordas of Nutley, New Jersey. "Mustard and dill enhance the flavor of this simple salad," Pat says.

Creamy Tomato Soup

2 tablespoons all-purpose flour
1 tablespoon sugar
2 cups milk, *divided*
4 cups tomato juice, heated
Chopped fresh parsley

In a large saucepan, combine flour, sugar and 1/4 cup milk; stir until smooth. Add remaining milk.

Bring to a boil over medium heat, stirring constantly. Cook and stir for 2 minutes or until thickened. Slowly stir in hot tomato juice until blended. Sprinkle with parsley. **Yield:** 4 servings.

Oatmeal Wheat Bread

✓ Uses less fat, sugar or salt. Includes Nutritional Analysis and Diabetic Exchanges.

1-3/4 cups boiling water
1 cup quick-cooking oats
1/2 cup molasses
1/4 cup shortening
1/4 cup orange juice
1-1/2 teaspoons salt
2 packages (1/4 ounce *each***) active dry yeast**
1/2 cup warm water (110° to 115°)
2-1/2 cups whole wheat flour
3 to 3-1/2 cups all-purpose flour
Melted stick margarine

In a large mixing bowl, combine boiling water, oats, molasses, shortening, orange juice and salt; let stand until warm (110°-115°). In a small bowl, dissolve the yeast in warm water; add to the oat mixture. Add the whole wheat flour and beat until

smooth. Add enough all-purpose flour to form a soft dough.

Turn onto a floured surface; knead until smooth and elastic, about 6-8 minutes. Place in a greased bowl, turning once to grease top. Cover and let rise in a warm place until doubled, about 1 hour.

Punch dough down. Shape into two loaves; place in greased 8-in. x 4-in. x 2-in. loaf pans. Cover and let rise until doubled, about 45 minutes. Bake at 350° for 40 minutes. Remove from pans; brush with margarine. Cool on wire racks. **Yield:** 2 loaves (32 slices).

Nutritional Analysis: One slice equals 121 calories, 110 mg sodium, 0 cholesterol, 23 g carbohydrate, 3 g protein, 2 g fat. **Diabetic Exchange:** 1-1/2 starch.

Tuna Pasta Salad

- 1 **package (7 ounces) small shell pasta,
  cooked and drained**
- 1 **can (6 ounces) tuna, drained and
  flaked**
- 1 **large carrot, shredded**
- 1/4 **cup chopped onion**
- 3/4 **cup mayonnaise**
- 1/4 **cup milk**
- 1 **tablespoon lemon juice**
- 2 **teaspoons prepared mustard**
- 1 **teaspoon dill weed**
- 1/2 **teaspoon salt**
- 1/8 **teaspoon pepper**

In a large salad bowl, combine pasta, tuna, carrot and onion. Combine remaining ingredients; whisk until smooth. Pour over pasta mixture and toss to coat. Cover and refrigerate for 1-2 hours. **Yield:** 4 servings.

Too Many Tomatoes?

If you find yourself with too many tomatoes to eat before they spoil, cook and freeze them. Then bring them out during the winter for a refreshing taste of summer!

When feeding a hungry horde, meat-and-potatoes meals are the mouth-watering mainstays in many kitchens across the country.

Just ask Carol Van Sickle, the Versailles, Kentucky cook who often puts together this low-budget but high-flavor menu for a group of family and friends at their request!

With the hearty ingredients packed into every bite, it will surely satisfy hungry appetites. Best of all, our Test Kitchen staff estimates that this economical dinner costs just $1.42 per setting.

Ham Loaves are a delicious way to dress up ham, and they also freeze well. Au Gratin Potatoes are real comfort food with their creamy cheese sauce. For a refreshing, slightly sweet side dish, Carol serves Orange Buttermilk Salad.

"Most everything in this meal can be prepared the day ahead, so I can enjoy the meal with my guests with no last-minute fuss in the kitchen," adds Carol.

She and her husband are originally from Pennsylvania and have two grown daughters.

Carol's satisfying spread here goes to show you don't have to forgo great flavor when eating inexpensively.

$1.42 Per Person

Ham Loaves

    4 eggs, lightly beaten
    1 cup milk
    4 cups dry bread crumbs
    2 pounds ground pork
    2 pounds ground fully cooked ham
1-1/2 cups packed brown sugar
    3/4 cup water
    1/2 cup vinegar
    1 teaspoon ground mustard

In a bowl, combine the eggs, milk and dry bread crumbs. Crumble ground pork and ham over mixture and mix well. Shape into 12 ovals, using 1 cup of mixture for each.

Place in an ungreased 15-in. x 10-in. x 1-in. baking pan. Combine brown sugar, water, vinegar and mustard; pour over the loaves.

Bake loaves, uncovered, at 350° for 1 hour and 15 minutes or until a meat thermometer reads 160-170°, basting every 15-20 minutes. **Yield:** 12 servings.

Au Gratin Potatoes

    8 cups cubed peeled potatoes
1/4 cup butter
    2 tablespoons all-purpose flour
    3/4 teaspoon salt
    1/8 teaspoon pepper
1-1/2 cups milk
    1 pound process American cheese, cubed
Minced fresh parsley

In a large saucepan, cook potatoes in boiling water until tender. Drain and place in a greased 2-1/2-qt. baking dish.

In a saucepan, melt butter. Add the flour, salt and pepper; stir to form a smooth paste. Gradually add milk, stirring constantly. Bring to a boil; boil and stir for 1 minute. Add cheese; stir just until melted.

Pour over potatoes. Cover and bake at 350° for 45-50 minutes or until bubbly. Sprinkle with parsley. **Yield:** 12 servings.

Orange Buttermilk Salad

**1 can (20 ounces) crushed pineapple,
    undrained**
1 package (6 ounces) orange gelatin
2 cups buttermilk
**1 carton (8 ounces) frozen whipped
    topping, thawed**

In a saucepan, bring the pineapple to a boil. Remove from the heat; add the gelatin and stir until dissolved. Add buttermilk and mix well. Cool to room temperature.

Fold in whipped topping. Pour into an 11-in. x 7-in. x 2-in. dish. Refrigerate several hours or overnight. Cut into squares. **Yield:** 12 servings.

Buttermilk Basics

As a substitute for each cup of buttermilk, place 1 tablespoon of lemon juice or vinegar in a measuring cup. Add milk to measure 1 cup. Let stand for 5 minutes before using in the recipe.

Buttermilk adds a delicious tang to baked goods, salad dressing, soups and sauces.

You can substitute buttermilk for regular milk in most baking recipes if you add 1/2 teaspoon baking soda for each cup of buttermilk to the dry ingredients.

After a long day at work, school or simply on the go, there's nothing like sitting down around the table to an old-fashioned, down-home dinner featuring great-tasting comfort foods.

Three busy cooks show how easy it is to assemble a million-dollar-tasting meal for just $1.37 per person.

Budget Macaroni and Cheese is a quick and creamy main dish shared by Debbie Carlson of San Diego, California. "I've tried many macaroni and cheese recipes over the years, but this is my favorite," she says. "It tastes so much better than the kind you make from a box mix."

Vegetable Salad from Pat Scott of Delray Beach, Florida is a super combination of crunchy fresh vegetables that are coated with a tangy mouth-watering marinade.

Even a budget meal can include dessert, points out Teresa Pelkey of Cherry Valley, Massachusetts, who sent her old-fashioned recipe for Great-Grandma's Ginger Cake. "The blend of spices is unbeatable," declares Teresa.

$1.37 Per Serving

Budget Macaroni and Cheese

> 1 package (7 ounces) elbow macaroni
> 3 tablespoons butter
> 3 tablespoons all-purpose flour
> 1/4 teaspoon salt
Dash pepper
> 1 cup milk
> 1 cup (4 ounces) shredded cheddar cheese

Cook the macaroni according to the package directions. Drain; set aside and keep warm. In a saucepan over medium-low heat, melt the butter. Add the flour, salt and pepper and stir to make a smooth paste.

Gradually add milk, stirring constantly. Heat and stir until thickened. Remove from the heat; stir in cheese until melted. Pour over macaroni and mix well. **Yield:** 4 servings.

Vegetable Salad

> 2 cups broccoli florets
> 2 cups cauliflowerets
> 4 large mushrooms, sliced
> 1 celery rib, sliced
> 1 medium green *or* sweet red pepper, diced
> 1/4 cup chopped onion
> 1/3 cup vegetable oil
> 1/4 cup sugar
> 1/4 cup vinegar

> 1/4 teaspoon salt
> 1-1/2 teaspoons poppy seeds

In a large bowl, combine the broccoli, cauliflower, mushrooms, celery, pepper and onion. Combine all of the remaining ingredients in a jar with tight-fitting lid and shake well. Pour over the vegetables and toss to coat. Cover and refrigerate 6-8 hours. **Yield:** 4 servings.

Great-Grandma's Ginger Cake

2-1/4 cups all-purpose flour
> 1 teaspoon baking soda
> 1 teaspoon ground ginger
> 1 teaspoon ground cinnamon
> 1/2 teaspoon salt

Dash ground cloves
  1/2 cup sugar
  1/2 cup shortening
  2/3 cup molasses
  1 egg
  3/4 cup boiling water
Whipped topping

Combine flour, baking soda, ginger, cinnamon, salt and cloves; set aside. In a mixing bowl, cream the sugar and shortening; beat in the molasses and egg. Stir in the dry ingredients alternately with water; mix well.

Pour into a greased 9-in. square baking pan. Bake at 350° for 35-40 minutes. Cool completely. Cut into squares; top with a dollop of whipped topping. Leftovers will keep several days in an airtight container. **Yield:** 9 servings.

Just Say 'Cheese'

Cheeses like cheddar, Swiss and Monterey Jack are easier to grate if they're cold. On the other hand, hard cheeses like Parmesan and Romano are easier to handle if they're at room temperature.

Firm and semifirm cheeses, like cheddar, can be grated ahead of time and refrigerated.

Cheese can turn stringy, rubbery or grainy when exposed to high heat. To avoid this, stir the cheese into a sauce toward the end of the cooking time and cook over low heat only until it melts.

Eat well economically at today's prices? You can! Three great cooks will help you plan a penny-pinching pizza party for your family, friends or a bunch of hungry kids. This savory Italian-style supper can be prepared for just $1.33 per setting.

Homemade Pizza, a hearty, zesty main dish with a crisp, golden crust, is shared by Marianne Edwards of Lake Stevens, Washington. Feel free to use whatever toppings your family enjoys.

Italian Salad from Regina Bianchi of Bessemer, Pennsylvania is super for summer with a light dressing and a nice combination of fresh ingredients.

For dessert, Leona Luecking of West Burlington, Iowa shares her extra-easy recipe for Berries in Custard Sauce. You can vary the recipe based on which berries you have on hand.

$1.33 Per Person

Homemade Pizza

1 package (1/4 ounce) active dry yeast
1 teaspoon sugar
1-1/4 cups warm water (110° to 115°)
1/4 cup vegetable oil
1 teaspoon salt
3-1/2 cups all-purpose flour
1/2 pound ground beef
1 small onion, chopped
1 can (15 ounces) tomato sauce
1 tablespoon dried oregano
1 teaspoon dried basil
1 medium green pepper, diced
2 cups (8 ounces) shredded mozzarella
  cheese

In large bowl, dissolve yeast and sugar in water; let stand for 5 minutes. Add oil and salt. Stir in flour, a cup at a time, to form soft dough. Turn onto a floured surface; knead until smooth and elastic, about 2-3 minutes. Place in greased bowl, turning once to grease top. Cover and let rise in a warm place until doubled, about 45 minutes.

Meanwhile, cook beef and onion over medium heat until meat is no longer pink; drain. Punch dough down; divide in half. Press each into a greased 12-in. pizza pan. Combine the tomato sauce, oregano and basil; spread over each crust. Top with beef mixture, green pepper and cheese. Bake at 400° for 25-30 minutes or until crust is lightly browned. **Yield:** 2 pizzas (6 servings).

Italian Salad

1/2 cup olive oil
1/4 cup cider vinegar
2 garlic cloves, minced
1 teaspoon sugar
1/2 teaspoon dried oregano
1/2 teaspoon salt
1/4 teaspoon pepper
1 small head lettuce, torn
1/2 cup sliced green onions
1/2 cup chopped celery
1/2 cup shredded mozzarella cheese
1 can (2-1/4 ounces) sliced ripe olives,
  drained
1 medium tomato, cut into wedges
2 tablespoons shredded Parmesan
  cheese

In a jar with tight-fitting lid, combine the first seven ingredients; shake well and set aside. In a large bowl, combine lettuce, onions, celery, mozzarella cheese, olives and tomato. Just before serving, add the dressing and toss. Sprinkle with Parmesan cheese. **Yield:** 6 servings.

Berries in Custard Sauce

1 cup milk
1 egg, lightly beaten
2 tablespoons sugar
Pinch salt
1/2 teaspoon vanilla extract
3 cups fresh blueberries, raspberries and
   strawberries

In saucepan, scald milk. Combine egg and sugar in a bowl; stir in small amount of hot milk. Return all to saucepan. Cook over low heat, stirring constantly, until mixture thickens slightly and coats a spoon, about 15 minutes. Remove from heat; stir in salt and vanilla. Chill at least 1 hour. Serve over berries. **Yield:** 6 servings.

Scalding Milk

Scalding milk was originally done to kill bacteria in milk—a process that's been rendered obsolete with pasteurization.

Today, scalding most often serves to speed preparation and cooking time—for instance, warm milk melts fat and dissolves sugar more quickly.

Before heating milk, rinse the pan with cold water to keep it from scorching and sticking. Cook it over medium heat, not high, or in a double boiler.

Whether she's looking to prepare an everyday meal for family or a special-occasion supper for friends and neighbors, Norma Erne of Albuquerque, New Mexico reaches for this delicious dinner that's fit for a king.

But don't think you have to spend a fortune to prepare this flavor-filled meal in your own kitchen. That's because our Test Kitchen staff estimates a cost of just $1.35 per setting.

Individual Meat Loaves are a fun way to serve an old standby. Says Norma, "I've made this hearty entree many times over the years, and it's always so good." Plus, these single-serving loaves bake much faster than one large loaf.

Zucchini Corn Medley, with its creamy cheese sauce and zippy taste, turns abundant garden vegetables into a comforting side dish.

Spiced Peaches are a delightful end to this delicious meal. "This is a super summer dessert when peaches are plentiful. The sweet chilled fruit topped with sour cream and brown sugar is so refreshing," Norma assures. When fresh peaches aren't available, use canned peach halves with tasty results.

$1.35 Per Serving

Individual Meat Loaves

  1 can (5 ounces) evaporated milk
  1 egg, lightly beaten
3/4 cup quick-cooking oats
1/4 cup chopped onion
  1 teaspoon salt
1/4 teaspoon pepper
1-1/2 pounds ground beef
1/3 cup ketchup
  1 tablespoon brown sugar
  1 tablespoon prepared mustard

In a bowl, combine the first six ingredients. Add beef and mix well. Shape into six loaves, about 4 in. x 2-1/2 in. Place in an ungreased 13-in. x 9-in. x 2-in. baking dish. Combine ketchup, sugar and mustard; spoon over loaves.

Bake, uncovered, at 350° for 35-45 minutes or until a meat thermometer reads 160° and no pink remains. **Yield:** 6 servings.

Zucchini Corn Medley

  5 medium zucchini, cut into 1/2-inch
    chunks
1/2 cup water
1/2 teaspoon salt
  1 package (10 ounces) frozen corn
  1 can (4 ounces) chopped green chilies
  2 tablespoons butter
  2 tablespoons all-purpose flour
1/4 teaspoon ground mustard

1/4 teaspoon salt
1/4 teaspoon pepper
  1 cup milk
1/2 cup shredded sharp cheddar cheese

In a saucepan over medium heat, cook the zucchini in water and salt until just tender, about 6 minutes. Add the corn; cook for 1 minute. Drain. Stir in the chilies and pour into a greased 1-1/2-qt. shallow baking dish.

Melt butter in a saucepan; stir in flour and seasonings until smooth and bubbly. Stir in milk; bring to a boil, stirring constantly. Boil 3-4 minutes or until thickened. Remove from the heat and stir in cheese until melted. Pour over vegetables.

Bake, uncovered, at 350° for 20 minutes or until bubbly. **Yield:** 6 servings.

Spiced Peaches

1/2 cup sugar
1/2 cup water
1/4 cup vinegar
8 to 10 whole cloves
1 cinnamon stick
6 fresh peaches, peeled and halved
1/2 cup sour cream
2 tablespoons brown sugar

In a large saucepan, bring the sugar, water, vinegar, cloves and cinnamon to a boil. Reduce the heat; simmer for 10 minutes. Add the peaches; simmer for about about 10 minutes or until heated through. Discard the cinnamon stick; pour mixture into a shallow baking dish.

Cover and chill 8 hours or overnight. Drain. Spoon peaches into serving dishes; garnish with a dollop of sour cream and sprinkle with brown sugar. **Yield:** 6 servings.

Eat Your Veggies!

Frozen vegetables such as corn and peas don't require thawing before being added to dishes like soups and casseroles. Such frozen vegetables can also be added to stir-frys and sautes, providing they'll be cooked long enough to thaw—usually only 1 to 2 minutes.

Dinner for less than a buck? Hard to believe, but three budget-conscious cooks prove that it's true! Our Test Kitchen home economists estimate that the total cost for their "soup-er" supper featured here is just 80¢ per serving.

Hearty Minestrone is a fresh-tasting main-dish soup that gets its zesty flavor from bulk Italian sausage. "When you want to use up your garden bounty of zucchini and green peppers, try this soup," advises cook Donna Smith of Victor, New York. If your family likes food extra spicy, use hot bulk Italian sausage instead.

For lightly sweet, biscuit-like rolls that are anything but dry, you can't beat simple Pop-Up Rolls. "With just four basic ingredients that are mixed in one bowl, they're so easy to make," assures Judi Brinegar of Liberty, North Carolina. "They go great served alongside just about everything."

Even an inexpensive meal doesn't have to go without a delectable dessert. Hazel Fritchie of Palestine, Illinois shares an old family recipe for Apple Nut Crunch, which has a wonderful aroma as it bakes in the oven. And its taste is even more terrific!

80¢ Per Person

Hearty Minestrone

    1 pound bulk Italian sausage
    2 cups sliced celery
    1 cup chopped onion
    6 cups chopped zucchini
    1 can (28 ounces) diced tomatoes,
        undrained
1-1/2 cups chopped green pepper
1-1/2 teaspoons Italian seasoning
1-1/2 teaspoons salt
    1 teaspoon dried oregano
    1 teaspoon sugar
  1/2 teaspoon dried basil
  1/4 teaspoon garlic powder

In a large saucepan, cook the sausage over medium heat until no longer pink. Remove with a slotted spoon to paper towels to drain, reserving 1 tablespoon of the drippings.
Saute celery and onion in the drippings for 5 minutes. Add sausage and remaining ingredients; bring to a boil. Reduce heat; cover and simmer for 20-30 minutes or until the vegetables are tender. **Yield:** 9 servings.

Pop-Up Rolls

1-1/2 cups self-rising flour
  3/4 cup milk
    3 tablespoons sugar
1-1/2 tablespoons mayonnaise

In a bowl, thoroughly combine all ingredients. Fill greased muffin cups half full. Bake at 375° for 18-20 minutes or until lightly browned. **Yield:** 9 rolls.
    Editor's Note: As a substitute for each cup of self-rising flour, place 1-1/2 teaspoons baking powder and 1/2 teaspoon salt in a measuring cup. Add all-purpose flour to measure 1 cup. For 1/2 cup, place 3/4 teaspoon baking powder and 1/4 teaspoon salt in a measuring cup. Add flour to measure 1/2 cup.
    Reduced-fat or fat-free mayonnaise may not be substituted for regular mayonnaise in this recipe.

Apple Nut Crunch

    1 egg
  3/4 cup sugar

1/3 cup all-purpose flour
1 teaspoon baking powder
1/8 teaspoon ground cinnamon
1/2 cup chopped peeled apple
1/2 cup chopped walnuts
1 teaspoon vanilla extract
2-1/4 cups ice cream

In a mixing bowl, beat the egg. In another bowl, combine sugar, flour, baking powder and ground cinnamon. Add to the egg and beat until smooth. Fold in the chopped apple, walnuts and vanilla extract.

Spoon mixture into a greased 8-in. square baking pan. Bake at 350° for 25-30 minutes or until a toothpick inserted near the center comes out clean. Cool. Serve with ice cream of your choice. **Yield:** 9 servings.

Smart Shopping

Before you go shopping, take a tour through your pantry and refrigerator. Be organized! Don't buy what's already hiding in your kitchen.

If you're a fan of coupons, remember this—it's not what you save, it's what you spend. If you save 30¢ on something you wouldn't ordinarily buy, you haven't really saved anything.

Never go to the store without a list. Buy only those items on your list; avoid impulse buys.

Shop after you've already eaten—never go to a grocery store hungry.

It's possible to save on your grocery bill without scrimping on good flavor when feeding your family. These recipes are suggested by three budget-minded cooks and combined by our Test Kitchen staff into a delicious meal you can serve for just $1.42 per person.

Honey Barbecued Chicken from Debbi Smith of Crossett, Arkansas has plenty of taste and eye appeal. It's baked to perfection in an onion sauce that's both sweet and spunky.

Flavored with garlic salt and chives, Party Potatoes are rich, creamy and oh, so yummy. A sprinkling of paprika gives this dish a festive look. Cyneli Fynaardt of Oskaloosa, Iowa submitted the recipe.

"I love German food, so I tried out the recipe for Sweet-Sour Beans and Carrots on my family and they really liked it," says Sherry DeHaan of Hays, Kansas. "I like to serve this side dish with German noodles and pork cutlets or a roast."

$1.42 Per Serving

Honey Barbecued Chicken

2 broiler/fryer chickens (3 pounds *each*), cut up
1/2 teaspoon salt
1/2 teaspoon pepper
2 large onions, chopped
2 cans (8 ounces *each*) tomato sauce
1/2 cup cider vinegar
1/2 cup honey
1/4 cup Worcestershire sauce
2 teaspoons paprika
1/2 teaspoon hot pepper sauce

Place chicken skin side down in an ungreased 13-in. x 9-in. x 2-in. baking dish. Sprinkle with salt and pepper. Combine the remaining ingredients; pour over chicken.

Bake, uncovered, at 375° for 30 minutes. Turn chicken and bake 20 minutes longer or until chicken juices run clear, basting occasionally with the sauce. **Yield:** 8 servings.

Party Potatoes

6 large potatoes, peeled and cubed
1 package (8 ounces) cream cheese, cubed
1 cup (8 ounces) sour cream
1/2 cup milk
1 teaspoon garlic salt
2 teaspoons minced chives
2 tablespoons butter, melted
1/2 teaspoon paprika

Place potatoes in a large saucepan and cover with water. Bring to a boil. Reduce heat; cover and cook for 15-20 minutes or until tender. Drain, then mash the potatoes. Beat in the cream cheese, sour cream, milk, garlic salt and chives; beat until well blended.

Transfer to a greased shallow 3-qt. baking dish. Drizzle potatoes with butter and sprinkle with paprika. Bake, uncovered, at 350° for 30-35 minutes or until edges are bubbly and potatoes are heated through. **Yield:** 8 servings.

Sweet-Sour Beans and Carrots

2 cups sliced carrots
4 cups frozen cut green beans
4 bacon strips, diced
2 medium onions, finely chopped

2 medium tart apples, peeled and diced
1/4 cup cider vinegar
2 tablespoons sugar
1 teaspoon salt

Place carrots in a large saucepan and cover with water. Bring to a boil. Cook, uncovered, for 4 minutes. Stir in beans. Return to a boil. Cook mixture 5-6 minutes longer or until the beans and carrots are tender. Drain.

In a large skillet, cook bacon over medium heat until crisp. Remove to paper towels to drain. Saute onions in drippings until tender. Add the apples, vinegar, sugar and salt; mix well. Cover and cook until apples are tender, about 2 minutes. Stir in the bean mixture; heat through. Sprinkle with bacon. **Yield:** 8 servings.

Frozen Assets

When fresh vegetables aren't in season, frozen vegetables are a convenient and nutritious option for budget-minded shoppers.

Store and generic brands often taste as good as name brands and usually cost less. Watch for coupons and in-store specials if you prefer name brands.

Flavor veggies with creamed soups, sauces or cheese…or mix them with noodles or grains such as rice. For example, create an inexpensive Italian dish by tossing cooked frozen vegetables with pasta and olive oil or tomato sauce and a sprinkling of Parmesan cheese.

Grocery budget a little tight? Don't worry! You can still enjoy satisfying foods that are full of flavor.

Three frugal cooks prove it with this mouth-watering meal that's perfect for a springtime luncheon or a light supper. Our Test Kitchen home economists estimate the total cost of this meal at just $1.73 per setting.

Canned salmon and frozen peas streamline the preparation of hearty Salmon Chowder from Pat Waymire from Yellow Springs, Ohio. Shredded Swiss and cheddar cheese, along with cauliflower and dill weed, add flavor to this appealing dish.

"I love my bread machine and am always trying new recipes in it," says Joy McMillan from The Woodlands, Texas. "Cracked Pepper Bread is one of my successes. When it's baking in the oven, the whole kitchen smells wonderful." Basil, garlic, chives and Parmesan cheese give this tall tender loaf a real Italian flavor.

Bernice Morris from Marshfield, Missouri dresses up her Garden Lettuce Salad with tomatoes, radishes, green onions, crisp bacon, hard-cooked eggs and a creamy homemade dressing. "It's a nice change from our usual wilted lettuce salad," she says. "This salad's also good with fried chicken and mashed potatoes or with a barbecue dinner."

$1.73 Per Person

Salmon Chowder

✓ Uses less fat, sugar or salt. Includes Nutritional Analysis and Diabetic Exchanges.

  1 cup thinly sliced green onions
  2 celery ribs, thinly sliced
  2 tablespoons butter
  2 tablespoons all-purpose flour
1/2 teaspoon salt
1/2 teaspoon dill weed
  4 cups milk
  2 cups cauliflowerets, cooked
  1 can (14-3/4 ounces) salmon, drained, skin and bones removed
  1 package (10 ounces) frozen peas, thawed
1/2 cup shredded Swiss cheese
1/2 cup shredded cheddar cheese

In a large saucepan, saute onions and celery in butter until tender. Stir in the flour, salt and dill until blended. Gradually add milk. Bring to a boil; cook and stir for 2 minutes or until thickened. Add the cauliflower, salmon and peas; heat through. Stir in the cheeses until melted. Serve immediately. **Yield:** 8 servings.

Nutritional Analysis: One 1-cup serving (prepared with fat-free milk and reduced-fat cheeses) equals 230 calories, 9 g fat (5 g saturated fat), 41 mg cholesterol, 558 mg sodium, 15 g carbohydrate, 3 g fiber, 22 g protein. **Diabetic Exchanges:** 2-1/2 lean meat, 1 starch.

Cracked Pepper Bread

1-1/2 cups water (70° to 80°)
  3 tablespoons olive oil
  3 tablespoons sugar
  2 teaspoons salt
  3 tablespoons minced chives
  2 garlic cloves, minced
  1 teaspoon garlic powder
  1 teaspoon dried basil
  1 teaspoon cracked black pepper
1/4 cup grated Parmesan cheese
  4 cups bread flour
2-1/2 teaspoons active dry yeast

In bread machine pan, place all ingredients in order suggested by manufacturer. Select basic bread setting. Choose crust color and loaf size if available.

Bake according to bread machine directions (check the dough after 5 minutes of mixing; add 1 to 2 tablespoons of water or flour if needed). **Yield:** 1 loaf (2 pounds).

Editor's Note: If your bread machine has a time-delay feature, we recommend you do not use it for this recipe.

Garden Lettuce Salad

5 cups torn leaf lettuce
2 medium tomatoes, chopped
3 hard-cooked eggs, sliced
3/4 cup sliced radishes
4 bacon strips, cooked and crumbled
3 green onions, sliced

DRESSING:
3/4 cup mayonnaise
1 tablespoon red wine vinegar
1 teaspoon lemon-lime soda
1/2 teaspoon salt
1/2 teaspoon sugar

In a salad bowl, toss the first six ingredients. In a small bowl, whisk the dressing ingredients. Serve with salad. **Yield:** 6 servings.

Don't Always Delay!

When using a time-delay feature, never use perishable ingredients, such as eggs, milk, cheese or meat, because they may spoil.

Eating well at today's prices isn't impossible. The frugal yet flavorful meal here combines recipes from three creative cooks. Our Test Kitchen staff estimates the total cost at just $1.56 per serving.

Traditional lasagna fixin's (minus the meat) make up Vegetable Noodle Bake, a satisfying casserole shared by Dixie Terry of Goreville, Illinois. The egg noodles are a great substitute for the usual lasagna noodles. "If you're out of hamburger, serve this dish and no one will even notice it's meatless because it's so tasty," Dixie assures.

Potato, tomato and onion complement the fresh green beans in colorful Green Bean Salad. A subtle oil-and-vinegar dressing lends fresh herb flavor to the mix. The refreshing recipe comes from the kitchen of Sarah Maranto of Bakersfield, California.

No one will be able to eat just one of Gail Wiese's yummy Chocolate Ribbon Bars, full of butterscotch, peanut butter and chocolate flavor. Unlike similar crispy cereal treats, these aren't sticky! "Over the years I've accumulated quite a few recipes from my co-workers, and this one is so easy to prepare," shares Gail from Athens, Wisconsin.

$1.56 Per Serving

Vegetable Noodle Bake

      1 can (14-1/2 ounces) whole tomatoes,
         drained and cut up
   3/4 cup canned tomato puree
   1/3 cup chopped onion
1-1/4 teaspoons dried oregano
   1/4 teaspoon garlic powder
   1/4 teaspoon salt
   1/8 teaspoon pepper
2-1/2 cups uncooked medium egg noodles
   1/2 cup small-curd cottage cheese
      1 package (10 ounces) frozen chopped
         spinach, thawed and squeezed dry
   1/3 cup shredded American cheese

In a large saucepan, combine the tomatoes, tomato puree, onion, oregano, garlic powder, salt and pepper. Bring to a boil. Reduce heat; simmer, uncovered, for 15 minutes. Meanwhile, cook noodles according to package directions; drain.

Spread 1/3 cup tomato mixture in a greased shallow 2-qt. baking dish. Top with half of the noodles. Spread with cottage cheese; top with spinach. Drizzle with 1/2 cup tomato mixture; top with remaining noodles and tomato mixture. Sprinkle with American cheese. Cover and bake at 350° for 20-25 minutes or until cheese is melted. **Yield:** 4 servings.

Green Bean Salad

☑ Uses less fat, sugar or salt. Includes Nutritional Analysis and Diabetic Exchanges.

      1 medium potato, peeled
   1/2 pound fresh green beans, cut
         into 2-inch pieces
      1 medium tomato, cubed
   1/2 small red onion, sliced and separated
         into rings
      2 tablespoons red wine vinegar
      2 tablespoons canola oil
      2 tablespoons minced fresh oregano
      2 tablespoons minced fresh parsley
   1/8 teaspoon salt

Place potato in a saucepan and cover with water. Bring to a boil; cook for 15 minutes or until tender. Drain and cool; cut into cubes. Place green beans in a saucepan and cover with water. Bring to a boil; cook, uncovered, for 6-8 minutes or until crisp-tender. Drain and cool.

In a serving bowl, combine beans, potato, tomato and onion. In a jar with a tight-fitting lid, combine the remaining ingredients; shake well. Pour over the bean mixture and toss to coat. **Yield:** 4 servings.

Nutritional Analysis: One serving (1 cup) equals 120 calories, 7 g fat (1 g saturated fat), 0 cholesterol, 81 mg sodium, 14 g carbohydrate, 3 g fiber, 3 g protein. **Diabetic Exchanges:** 1 vegetable, 1 fat, 1/2 starch.

Chocolate Ribbon Bars

1 package (10 to 11 ounces) butterscotch chips
1 cup peanut butter
8 cups crisp rice cereal
2 cups (12 ounces) semisweet chocolate chips

1/4 cup butter, cubed
2 tablespoons water
3/4 cup confectioners' sugar

In a large microwave-safe bowl, melt butterscotch chips and peanut butter; stir until smooth. Gradually stir in cereal until well coated. Press half of the mixture into a greased 13-in. x 9-in. x 2-in. pan; set remaining mixture aside.

In another large microwave-safe bowl, melt semisweet chips and butter. Stir in water until blended. Gradually add the confectioners' sugar, stirring until smooth.

Spread over cereal layer. Cover and refrigerate for 10 minutes or until chocolate layer is set. Spread remaining cereal mixture over the top. Chill before cutting. **Yield:** 2 dozen.

Editor's Note: Reduced-fat or generic brands of peanut butter are not recommended for this recipe.

Looking for ways to save on your grocery bill while still serving your family delicious and nutritious meals? Leave it to *Taste of Home* subscribers to come up with some taste-tempting solutions!

Our Test Kitchen home economists have put together this satisfying meal with recipes from three of our subscribers. It makes a filling lunch or a light summer supper...for just 99¢ per person.

For her Tuna Cheese Melts, Bernadine Dirmeyer of Harpster, Ohio dresses up a typical tuna sandwich with American cheese and rye bread spread with a mixture of sour cream and garlic salt. Cooked in a skillet, this sandwich oozes with flavor.

Radish Potato Salad from Lydia Garcia of Hanover, Pennsylvania is well coated with a creamy dill dressing. This summery salad, made with radish slices and chopped eggs, is not only pretty but easy to prepare, too.

"Cinnamon-Sugar Crisps are a favorite with children...and adults, too," says Kim Marie Van Rheenen of Mendota, Illinois. These sweet and spicy refrigerator cookies go great with a cup of coffee or a cold glass of milk. You won't be able to eat just one!

Tuna Cheese Melts

1/2 cup sour cream
1/2 teaspoon garlic salt
8 slices light rye bread
1 can (6 ounces) tuna, drained
2 tablespoons mayonnaise
4 slices process American cheese
4 tablespoons butter, *divided*

Combine sour cream and garlic salt; spread on one side of each slice of bread. In a small bowl, combine tuna and mayonnaise; spread on four slices of bread. Top with cheese and remaining bread; gently press together.

Melt 2 tablespoons butter in a large skillet over medium heat. Add two sandwiches; cook until both sides are golden brown and cheese is melted. Repeat with remaining butter and sandwiches. **Yield:** 4 servings.

Radish Potato Salad

5 medium red potatoes (about 1-1/2 pounds)
1 cup sliced radishes
2 hard-cooked eggs, chopped
3/4 cup mayonnaise
3 tablespoons minced fresh dill *or* **2 teaspoons dill weed**
2 tablespoons cider vinegar
1 tablespoon sugar

1/4 teaspoon salt
Dash pepper

Place the potatoes in a saucepan and cover with water. Bring to a boil. Reduce heat; cover and cook for 15-20 minutes or until the potatoes are tender. Drain and cool.

Peel and cube potatoes; place in a large bowl. Add radishes and eggs. In a small bowl, combine the mayonnaise, dill, vinegar, sugar, salt and pepper. Gently fold into potato mixture. Cover and refrigerate for at least 1 hour. **Yield:** 4 servings.

Cinnamon-Sugar Crisps

3/4 cup butter, softened
1/3 cup sugar

1/3 cup packed brown sugar
1 egg
1 teaspoon vanilla extract
1-3/4 cups all-purpose flour
1 teaspoon ground cinnamon
1/4 teaspoon salt
2 tablespoons colored sprinkles

In a mixing bowl, cream butter and sugars. Beat in egg and vanilla. Combine the flour, cinnamon and salt; gradually add to creamed mixture. Shape into a 12-in. roll; wrap in plastic wrap. Refrigerate for 2 hours or until firm.

Unwrap and cut into 1/4-in. slices. Place 2 in. apart on ungreased baking sheets. Decorate with sprinkles. Bake at 350° for 10-12 minutes or until lightly browned. Remove to wire racks to cool.
Yield: 3-1/2 dozen.

Versatile Tuna

Tuna salad is both thrifty to make and fun to eat. Try out these ideas to add variety to this popular dish.

Make your favorite tuna salad recipe and spread it on a tortilla. Add chopped tomato and lettuce, roll up and serve.

Instead of adding diced pickles or sweet relish to your tuna salad, spice up the mixture with diced jalapenos and chopped green onions.

For a tasty twist, add chopped black olives and a dash of lemon-pepper seasoning to the tuna salad.

Grocery shopping can make you nervous—especially if you're on a tight budget but still want to serve your family mouth-watering meals.

We're here to tell you that you can be frugal and satisfy hearty appetites at dinnertime. Three cooks prove it with these penny-pinching yet palate-pleasing dishes compiled by our Test Kitchen home economists. They estimate the total cost for this meal at just $1.11 a serving!

Great Northern Bean Stew is thick with beans, tomatoes, carrots, cabbage, onion and pork sausage, which lends just the right amount of spicy flavor. "A bowlful of this filling dish is guaranteed to chase the winter chills away," says Mildred Sherrer of Bay City, Texas.

"We love popovers at our house, but after a while they taste a little flat...so I added a few herbs to sparkle them up a bit," says Lorraine Caland of Thunder Bay, Ontario. "I like to serve Herbed Popovers for brunch or with a roast beef dinner."

Hoosier Cream Pie ends a meal on a cozy comforting note. This traditional banana cream pie with its meringue topping is so pretty to look at and cuts nicely, too.

"My grandmother also used her recipe to make coconut pie and butterscotch pie," recalls Edna Hoffman of Hebron, Indiana.

$1.11 Per Serving

Great Northern Bean Stew

1 pound bulk pork sausage
1 cup chopped onion
1 can (28 ounces) diced tomatoes, undrained
1 can (15-1/2 ounces) great northern beans, rinsed and drained
2 cups chopped cabbage
1 cup sliced carrots
1 tablespoon white vinegar
1 tablespoon brown sugar
1/2 teaspoon salt
1/2 teaspoon dried thyme
1/2 teaspoon paprika
1/2 teaspoon pepper
1/4 teaspoon hot pepper sauce
2 tablespoons minced fresh parsley

In a large saucepan, cook the sausage and onion over medium heat until the meat is no longer pink; drain. Add the next 11 ingredients. Bring to a boil.

Reduce heat; cover and simmer for 50-60 minutes or until vegetables are tender. Stir in parsley; cook 5 minutes longer. **Yield:** 6 servings.

Herbed Popovers

1 cup all-purpose flour
1 teaspoon dried thyme
1 teaspoon dried basil
1 teaspoon rubbed sage
1/4 teaspoon celery salt
3 eggs
1 cup milk
1 tablespoon vegetable oil

In a bowl, combine the flour, thyme, basil, sage and celery salt. In another bowl, combine the eggs, milk and oil, then whisk into the dry ingredients just until blended (the batter will be lumpy). Refrigerate for 30 minutes.

Fill eight greased and floured 6-oz. custard cups half full. Place on a baking sheet. Bake at 450° for 15 minutes.

Reduce heat to 350° (do not open oven door). Bake 15-20 minutes longer or until deep golden brown (do not underbake). Serve immediately. **Yield:** 8 popovers.

Hoosier Cream Pie

3/4 cup sugar
1/4 cup cornstarch
1/4 teaspoon salt
2-1/2 cups milk
   3 egg yolks, lightly beaten
   2 tablespoons butter
1-1/2 teaspoons vanilla extract
   3 medium firm bananas
   1 pastry shell (9 inches), baked
MERINGUE:
   3 egg whites
1/4 teaspoon cream of tartar
   6 tablespoons sugar

In a saucepan, combine the sugar, cornstarch and salt. Stir in milk until smooth. Cook and stir over medium-high heat until thickened and bubbly. Reduce heat; cook and stir for 2 minutes. Remove from the heat.

Stir a small amount of hot filling into egg yolks; return all to the pan. Bring to a gentle boil; cook and stir for 2 minutes. Stir in butter and vanilla until butter is melted; keep warm. Slice bananas into the pastry shell.

In a mixing bowl, beat egg whites and cream of tartar on medium speed until soft peaks form. Gradually beat in sugar, 1 tablespoon at a time, on high until stiff glossy peaks form and sugar is dissolved. Pour hot filling over bananas. Spread meringue evenly over filling, sealing edges to crust.

Bake at 350° for 15 minutes or until the meringue is golden brown. Cool the pie on a wire rack for 1 hour. Refrigerate for at least 3 hours before serving. Store the leftovers in the refrigerator. **Yield:** 6-8 servings.

Serving brunch dishes for supper...and on a budget? You bet!

Three frugal cooks prove it with this mouth-watering meal that's perfect for Sunday brunch or a light supper. Our Test Kitchen home economists estimate the cost at just $1.19 per setting.

"I love serving foods that both complement and contrast each other, like my Garlic Zucchini Frittata," relates Michelle Krzmarzick of Redondo Beach, California. "This flavorful egg dish can be made in minutes and easily doubled. Sometimes I use leftover taco meat or chopped ham instead of bacon."

Elizabeth Hunter of Prosperity, South Carolina blends orange marmalade with sour cream and mayonnaise for her zesty Fresh Fruit Dip. It's a real refresher!

Cinnamon Muffins, with a dash of nutmeg in the batter, are seasoned to please. "My husband grew up enjoying these tender, yummy muffins that his mother made on special weekend mornings," says Katherine McVey from Raleigh, North Carolina.

$1.19 Per Person

Garlic Zucchini Frittata

- 1 tablespoon butter
- 1 tablespoon finely chopped onion
- 4 garlic cloves, minced
- 1 medium zucchini, shredded
- 6 eggs
- 1/4 teaspoon ground mustard
- 4 bacon strips, cooked and crumbled
- 1/4 teaspoon salt
- 1/8 teaspoon pepper
- 1/4 cup shredded Swiss cheese
- 1/4 cup sliced green onions

In a 10-in. ovenproof skillet, melt butter over medium-high heat. Add onion and garlic; saute for 1 minute. Add zucchini; cook for 3 minutes or until tender.

In a bowl, beat eggs and mustard. Pour into skillet. Sprinkle with bacon, salt and pepper. As eggs set, lift edges, letting uncooked portion flow underneath. Cook until eggs are nearly set, about 7 minutes. Meanwhile, preheat broiler.

Place skillet under the broiler, 6 in. from the heat, for 30-60 seconds or until the eggs are completely set. Sprinkle with cheese and green onions. Broil 30 seconds longer or until cheese is melted. Cut into wedges. **Yield:** 4 servings.

Fresh Fruit Dip

- 1/2 cup mayonnaise
- 1/2 cup sour cream
- 1/3 cup orange marmalade
- 1 tablespoon milk
- 1/2 pound green grapes
- 1/2 pound strawberries

In a small bowl, whisk the mayonnaise, sour cream, marmalade and milk. Refrigerate until serving. Serve with grapes and strawberries or the fresh fruit of your choice. **Yield:** 1-1/3 cups.

Cinnamon Muffins

- 1/3 cup shortening
- 1/2 cup sugar
- 1 egg
- 1-1/2 cups all-purpose flour
- 1-1/2 teaspoons baking powder

1/2 teaspoon salt
1/4 teaspoon ground nutmeg
1/2 cup milk
TOPPING:
1/2 cup sugar
1-1/2 teaspoons ground cinnamon
3 tablespoons butter, melted

In a bowl, cream shortening and sugar. Add egg; beat well. Combine the flour, baking powder, salt and nutmeg; add to creamed mixture alternately with milk and mix well.

Fill greased muffin cups half full. Bake at 350° for 15-20 minutes or until a toothpick inserted near the center comes out clean.

In a shallow bowl, combine sugar and cinnamon. Dip muffin tops in butter, then in cinnamon-sugar. Serve warm. **Yield:** 1 dozen.

Dip Into Dips

Be budget-minded and buy fresh fruit in season (strawberries in late spring, raspberries in summer, etc). Then serve it for dessert with an easy-to-make and economical dip.

Combine a jar of marshmallow creme and a package of cream cheese and stir in a splash of orange juice to taste.

Or add a bit of brown sugar and a dash of cinnamon and nutmeg to custard-style vanilla yogurt.

Both of these dips are simple to make, easy on the pocketbook and taste great!

Stretch Your Budget Even Further by
CLIPPING COUPONS

Saving money is the main reason most people use coupons on groceries. Those cents-off coupons add up to real dollars in almost no time.

Coupons also offer a financial enticement to try products you might not otherwise buy. It's often fun to try something new, and today's experiment can easily become a mainstay if you and your family like the product.

Here are some tips to get the most out of the time you spend clipping, sorting and organizing your coupons before you head to the supermarket:

- If you have the time, clip a coupon that interests you as soon as you see it. Then you won't forget. If you're too busy at that moment, put it in a pile for your next coupon-clipping session.

- Look for coupons in magazines, newspapers and flyers. Mention to your friends and neighbors that you're a couponer. You'll be surprised how many people will volunteer to save the Sunday newspaper coupon sections for you. Unused coupon inserts may also be available at your neighborhood recycling center.

- At least once a week, sort through your coupon pile and clip what you want. If you wait longer, the pile may become too daunting and some coupons may have already expired.

- When clipping coupons, be careful not to cut off the expiration date and any part of the UPC bar code. Some stores reject coupons missing this information.

- Devise a system for sorting coupons. If you always shop at the same store, you can organize by aisle. If not, organize by type of product. Use simple, functional dividers such as canned goods, cereal, coffee, frozen, fruit, laundry, medication, paper products, etc.

- You can buy a coupon organizer or make your own using envelopes or a small shoe box and cardboard dividers. Put your titled dividers in alphabetical order so it's easy to find the category you need.

- Organize your coupons within the dividers by expiration date, with the ones that expire first being closest to the front. You may even want to keep a special envelope or divider labeled "coupons that expire within the next month". That way you won't miss out on the savings.

- Before you sit down to draft your grocery list, write down what meals you plan to make, taking advantage of store specials, your coupons and what's already in your cupboard. Put the coupons that you'll need for your shopping trip together in one envelope.

- You may want to shop alone to eliminate distractions. Go at a time when you'll avoid crowds and shelf stocking (when the aisles are likely to be full of boxes).

- Ask your cashier how you should present the coupons: in a group before the sale is rung up, after all the items are tallied or as each item is rung up, matching each product with its coupon. Be friendly and patient and the cashier will be, too.

- After you've established your couponing routine, look for opportunities to trade coupons with others. If a product you like has an 800 number on the back, call and ask to be placed on the promotion list.

- Be on the lookout for stores that feature double-coupon days.

- Consider taking along your coupon file when you go shopping. An unadvertised in-store special may combine nicely with a coupon, offering you extra money off the item.

- If you still wonder if couponing is worth the effort, put all your coupon "savings" into an envelope or piggy bank for a few weeks. You'll be surprised how quickly you've accumulated enough money to pay for an evening out or another special treat.

INDEX

✓ Recipe includes Nutritional Analysis and Diabetic Exchanges.